# CROSSING THE GOAL

DANNY ABRAMOWICZ

# CROSSING THE GOAL

*A Saint Goes Marching On*

EWTN PUBLISHING, INC.
Irondale, Alabama

EWTN Publishing, Inc.
5817 Old Leeds Road, Irondale, AL 35210

Distributed by Sophia Institute Press
Box 5284, Manchester, NH 03108

Library of Congress Cataloging-in-Publication Data

Names: Abramowicz, Danny, author.
Title: Crossing the goal : a saint goes marching on! / Danny Abramowicz.
Description: Irondale, Alabama : EWTN Pub., Inc., 2016.
Identifiers: LCCN 2016021410 | ISBN 9781682780183 (pbk. : alk. paper)
Subjects: LCSH: Abramowicz, Danny. | Catholics—United States—Biography. |
    Men—Religious life. | Prayer—Catholic Church. | Spiritual life—Catholic
    Church. | Football players—United States—Biography. | Football
    coaches—United States—Biography.
Classification: LCC BX4705.A2265 A3 2016 | DDC 282.092 [B]—dc23
LC record available at https://lccn.loc.gov/2016021410

First printing

*To my wife of fifty years*
*and my best friend—Claudia*

# CONTENTS

# FOREWORD

The first time I saw Danny Abramowicz was November 5, 1972, at Metropolitan Stadium in Bloomington, Minnesota. Danny's New Orleans Saints were in town to play the Minnesota Vikings. I was fifteen years old, and, like most Minnesota boys my age, I was a big Vikings fan. I have two distinct memories from that game. First, the front four of the Vikings' defense, known then as the Purple People Eaters, spent most of the game in the Saints' backfield. Second, the play of number 46, wide receiver Danny Abramowicz, left a deep impression on me. He was a bit of an anomaly—a short, gritty, hardnosed receiver who, despite having only average speed, had a knack for getting open and catching every ball thrown his way.

The Saints lost that game, but my brother and I liked the way Danny played. He was tough, and he threw himself into the game with reckless abandon. We liked him so much that we kept his football card in our NFL players' collection. Little did I know then that almost thirty-two years later our paths would converge in a shared passion to reach men for Jesus Christ and His Church.

Danny and I first met at a men's conference where we were both speakers. Once again he left an impression on me and on every other man at the conference. Just minutes into his talk I knew he was not your typical celebrity athlete speaker. He told a few funny NFL stories to get our attention, but then he grabbed our hearts with the honest and transparent way he talked about his own life—his successes and his failures. Then he spoke about Jesus—no nonsense and straight from the heart with a manly conviction that was contagious. The men were locked into Danny's every word. He challenged us that day to change our lives, to stand up and to man up and to enter the spiritual battle that is raging against our families and the Church.

Danny is a man on a mission. The Lord has called him to reach men, especially the many who were baptized Catholic but have become disengaged from the Faith. Most of these men have no idea what they're missing. Danny understands the position they're in because for many years he lived just that way. He had little time for the things of God because he was convinced that what he had—fame, success, and money—were the things in which we find happiness in this life. As he puts it, he was passionately committed to feeding his ego, which led him to alcohol addiction and an unmanageable life. Despite all that he achieved, he was left empty—a broken man living a lie. It was there, in that place, in the darkness and shame, that Danny found the power to begin to step into the light of God's truth and mercy. He knows how men struggle; he knows the battles we face; and he knows that Jesus is the answer to the deepest longing of every man's heart.

For the past ten years I've had the privilege, along with Curtis Martin, the founder of the Fellowship of Catholic University Students (FOCUS), and Brian Patrick, host of *EWTN News Nightly*, to work closely with Danny on the television program *Crossing the Goal*. The program was an idea that came to Danny in prayer. I think I can speak for Curtis and Brian when I say that our time together as a team under Danny's leadership has been a rich experience of the joy of brotherhood in Christ. Each of us owes a debt of gratitude to Danny for the friendship, mentoring, and support we received from him. The closer we got to Danny, the more we could see the depth of his faith, his passion for Jesus and the Church, his dedication to his lovely wife, Claudia, and their family, and the total commitment he has made to walk the walk. Danny is the real deal.

I am delighted that Danny decided to write this book. It is vintage Danny. It's an honest, straightforward account of an amazing life. The book will make you laugh and cry. It's fundamentally a story of redemption, forgiveness, and God's power to heal marriages and families. It's a beautiful testimony to the truth that Jesus Christ is alive, that He is acting in the present, and that He is changing lives.

Finally, I just want to say thank you to Claudia. There would be no redemptive story to tell without Claudia. Although most of the story in this book is about Danny, Claudia's faith, fidelity, and forgiving heart made up the soil in which the seed of God's redemptive work was first planted in their marriage. Danny and Claudia together are witnesses to hope.

— Peter Herbeck

# CROSSING THE GOAL

# MY QUEST FOR HOLINESS

For many years I have been on a quest for holiness. From my wife, Claudia, to my children, my extended family, and my friends from ministries and small groups across America, I have had many wonderful companions on this trek. The purpose of this book is to bring you along on my journey. There are joyful moments and sorrowful moments, moments filled with the Holy Spirit and moments filled with despair. Even though much of my story takes place in front of the backdrop of professional football, my spiritual journey is similar to so many others' across the country and the world. My hope is that my story will help you to understand your journey and inspire you to undertake your own quest for holiness.

Holiness can't just be one quest among many for us; it is, in the end, the only quest that matters. I went on quests for popularity and money and accolades and alcohol throughout my life, as we will see, but only growing in holiness has brought me lasting peace.

Let's start, though, with three extraordinary events in the life of my family that show where that quest led us spiritually — and where, God willing, it can lead you, too.

## Polish Pilgrimage

As I sit down to write about the Pope John Paul II pilgrimage we took to Poland, I notice that today is his feast day! See how the Lord works! Pope St. John Paul II is my hero and the patron saint of the Crossing the Goal ministry (more on that later). I always wanted to visit Poland to follow in his footsteps. When I discovered that Franciscan University of Steubenville was offering a Pope St. John Paul II pilgrimage to Poland led by Bishop David Zubik of Pittsburgh, Claudia and I immediately signed up.

Our first destination was Czestochowa, a city in southern Poland, to visit the monastery and shrine of Our Lady of Czestochowa, also known the Black Madonna for the dark color of this incredible icon. I felt as though my grandmother — my Babka — were there with me because she had a great devotion to Our Lady of Czestochowa. Bishop Zubik celebrated Mass in the small chapel in front of the original painting of Our Lady. The icon is shown only once a day, and it is absolutely beautiful; I was deeply moved each time I looked up at her.

There were so many places in Poland that left a deep impression on us, including Wadowice — the hometown of John Paul II. Here we celebrated Mass in the small parish church where Karol Wojtyla, as he was known before his papacy, was an altar server. During Mass I couldn't stop thinking about how this little village produced the holy man who would have such a tremendous impact on the world. It is obvious that God's hand was on young Karol from the start.

Next we traveled to Kraków, a large, old, and very picturesque city. I think Kraków represents the true Poland rather than Warsaw, which was destroyed during World War II and totally rebuilt with modern architecture under the influence of communism. Kraków has many large and beautiful Catholic churches, and when we went into the cathedral, the guide pointed out to us the very pew where Archbishop Karol Wojtyla would pray for hours.

Just outside Kraków is the Divine Mercy Shrine and Convent dedicated to St. Faustina, whose visions of Jesus brought us the Divine Mercy devotion. Since the Divine Mercy Chaplet had become one of our favorite prayers, it was a true blessing that we were able to join the sisters in praying it. We were then able to remain in the chapel afterward to pray and meditate.

We also visited Auschwitz, which was simply overwhelming. The feeling of the evil, demonic forces at work there left all of us in the tour shaken. Although there were hundreds of people from all over the world going through the camp, there was complete silence. Our group stopped to pray quietly at the cell of St. Maximilian Kolbe, a priest who was sentenced to death by starvation after offering his life in place of another man's.

It was such a blessing to be able to go on that Polish pilgrimage. Our Faith has so many beautiful stories to tell and places to visit; Claudia and I felt so fortunate to have grown in appreciation of the Catholic Faith so that we could enjoy such a trip to the fullest. But even Poland can't quite match the history in the Holy Land.

## Bringing the Gospels to Life

Claudia and I had always wanted to visit the Holy Land, and although turmoil in the Middle East almost stopped us, we ended up taking the trip in the summer of 2014. We flew into Tel Aviv and then boarded a bus for a several-hour trip to our hotel on the banks of the Sea of Galilee. All of the sites we visited were incredible, but I will share only a few of them here.

On the first morning, we went to the exact location where Jesus gave His sermon on the Beatitudes, overlooking the Sea of Galilee, and a priest in our group celebrated Mass. We also had an opportunity to swim in the Sea of Galilee, which is actually quite small, and to float in the Dead Sea. We hear about places like the Sea of Galilee in the Gospels, but they can seem like places in stories from another world. To swim in the waters on which Jesus walked truly brought His story to life for us.

Later, we traveled to Cana, home of the wedding feast where Jesus' public ministry began, where we had Mass and renewed our wedding vows. Then we went up the Mount of the Transfiguration and down to the Jordan River (which is only twenty or thirty yards wide) to renew our baptismal vows. It was incredibly moving to say the words of these vows in places that were meaningful to our Lord.

Before leaving this region of Israel, we traveled to the Golan Heights to visit some holy sites. Our guide also wanted us to go to the top of Mount Hermon to see the beautiful view of the Hula Valley that borders Syria, but when we arrived, we noticed several UN and Israeli soldiers. As we looked out over the valley, we could hear gunfire and explosions. The UN forces informed us that ISIS was attacking a Syrian village. It felt surreal to be that close to a war we usually see only on television. All of us began to pray, as we knew that people were dying within earshot of us. It was very quiet on the bus home as everyone prayed the Rosary.

We then traveled to Jerusalem and visited the Holy Sepulchre, where we said evening prayers with the Franciscan Friars, after which we had an opportunity to enter Jesus' tomb—the very place where He rose from the dead!—for a short visit and prayer. The next morning, we went back and had Mass at the tomb; the two priests who accompanied us on the pilgrimage prayed the Eucharistic Prayer inside the tomb. After Mass we walked to Calvary, where we each had an opportunity to venerate the spot where the Cross had been placed—where our Lord had died.

The next morning, we arose very early and went back to the Old City so we could pray the Stations of the Cross in peace. The last place we visited was the Upper Room. As we prayed aloud, I tried to visualize what it must have been like for the Apostles at the Last Supper with Jesus and what it was like when the Holy Spirit came down upon them at Pentecost. I can only imagine their feelings, but being in that room made me feel close to them in a unique and unforgettable way.

When I returned home to Chicago, at the first Mass I attended the Gospel reading was on the Beatitudes. That reading came alive for me as never before, because I had participated in a Mass that was celebrated on the spot where Jesus had delivered that message. Ever since our trip to the Holy Land, the Holy Scriptures have become more meaningful to me. It is one thing to read and to hear the stories of Jesus' life, but to see the places where they happened made the Gospel stories more real to me than ever before. Nothing brings our Faith to life quite like a visit to the Holy Land.

## Closer to Home

Finally I would like to share with you an event that turned out to be just the beginning of an ongoing spiritual journey. More than twenty-five years ago, I was touched by the writings of Thomas

Merton, the American Trappist monk best known for his book *The Seven Storey Mountain*. Recently Pope Francis mentioned him, along with Dorothy Day, as a wonderful example of American Catholicism. I was so intrigued by Merton that Claudia and I decided to visit Gethsemani, the Trappist monastery in Kentucky where he spent much of his life.

On the first evening of our visit, after night prayers, the abbot made an announcement that one of the monks would be giving a short reflection in a small chapel. Shortly before the reflection was to begin, a monk sat down next to me. After the reflection, he introduced himself to me as Brother Giuseppe, from Steubenville, Ohio. Claudia and I immediately shared with him that we were born and raised there as well! It turned out that he knew my parents when they were children, but he had left Steubenville when he was sixteen to enter Gethsemani.

I don't think this was a coincidence; God meant for this to happen. We have visited Gethsemani several times, and Brother Giuseppe has told us stories about Thomas Merton, whom he knew personally. We still correspond with Brother Giuseppe, who is now quite old.

That first visit more than twenty-five years ago started us on a spiritual journey to monasteries throughout the country, such as the Abbey of the Genesee in New York, New Melleray Monastery in Iowa, Holy Angels Monastery in Oregon, and Saint Meinrad Monastery in Indiana. Each time we visit one of these monasteries, we realize that we have been on holy ground and that we have been fed spiritually. You don't have to travel overseas to have an enlightening out-of-the-ordinary spiritual experience; there are beautiful monasteries and abbeys all around the United States. The devotion of the men and women who live in religious communities is truly an inspiration.

## Back to the Beginning

These spiritual experiences have helped us grow in our love of God and His Church. But before I could appreciate these wonders, I first needed to accept Jesus Christ in my life. The truth is that for much of my life — including some of the most "successful" moments when I was winning awards and hanging out with the elite of New Orleans — I would have laughed at the idea of going on a pilgrimage or visiting a monastery. How did I get from there to here? That's what the rest of this book is about.

# CHAPTER 1
# GROWING UP

I was born on Friday, July 13, 1945, in Steubenville, Ohio, to Dorothy "Dot" and Stanley "Paper" Abramowicz. My Friday-the-thirteenth birthday should have signaled right away that I was going to be a handful! My brother, Joe "Little Brush," came later. Steubenville might be the nickname capital of America; just in my circles I knew guys who went by Slugs, Pokey, Pepper, Goose, Ironhead, Carp, Brassy, Feets, and Melonhead, to name a few.

Steubenville is (or, more accurately, used to be) a steel-mill and coal-mining town on the banks of the Ohio River. A ten-mile stretch of highway links Steubenville with Western Pennsylvania, with the West Virginia panhandle in between. The river separates Steubenville from its West Virginian sister, Weirton.

When I was growing up, Steubenville was dominated by Italian, Polish, and Irish immigrants; my parents' families were of Polish and Irish descent. My dad worked as a fireman for thirty-five years, retiring with the rank of captain. During most of my childhood, we lived in either a rental property or on the bottom floor of my great-grandparents' home.

Finally, in my early high school years, we were able to purchase a small fixer-upper house, but it required a lot of work, which my brother and I dreaded. Neither of us was very handy, and we knew we would get stuck with the grunt work. Our dad, on the other hand, was really good with tools, but he wouldn't be able to handle this job alone, so some family members and firemen helped the cause. The Steubenville I grew up in was the kind of place where neighbors helped neighbors without needing to be asked.

Back in those days, the work schedule for firemen was twenty-four hours on duty and forty-eight hours off duty. My dad had to pick up spare jobs during his downtime, as the fireman's pay was not sufficient to cover the bills. He would drag me and my brother along to his regular handyman jobs, where I really learned to respect my dad's work ethic. Even so, I told myself that when I grew up, I absolutely did not want to do manual labor for a living.

## A (Somewhat) Catholic Upbringing

I was raised in the Roman Catholic Church and attended Catholic schools. The Dominican nuns who taught me lived in a large convent connected to the grade school. They all wore white habits with rosary beads dangling from a black belt around the waist and long black-and-white veils that covered all of their hair; all we could see was their faces. The sisters could never sneak up on us because those rosary beads would jangle together, banging against the desks in the narrow classroom rows.

Most of the parishes and grade schools in Steubenville were built around ethnic neighborhoods. For instance, our parish and school, St. Peter's, was Irish; the Polish parish was St. Stanislaus; and the Italian one was St. Anthony. On my dad's side of the family, all the children attended St. Stanislaus, and on my mom's side, all the kids attended St. Peter's.

Our entire family lived within a two-mile radius, so almost all of our social life was built around family activities such as picnics, birthday parties, family meals, and church events. It was common for family and friends to drop by unexpectedly.

The Irish side of the family would all meet for 10 a.m. Mass at St. Peter's then load up with ice, snacks, pop (that's soda, for you non-Midwesterners), and, of course, plenty of beer for a picnic at the lake. We didn't get together with the Polish side too often, but when we did, it was really special. We would go to my grandmother "Babka" Abramowicz's house on Sunday afternoon for a large family meal of authentic Polish food. After a Polish prayer, we would all stuff ourselves, always leaving room for the Old World desserts.

My Babka was an excellent cook, but more importantly she was one of the gentlest and holiest people I have ever met. I rarely saw her without a rosary in her hand, and she seemed to be in total peace. She would always say to my brother and me, "You are good boys." She found what was good in everybody!

As I grew older I tried to figure out what made her so gentle and peaceful. Much of her childhood was spent trying to cope with life under communism and Nazism. Finally, at the age of eighteen, she was able to immigrate to the United States using money from her brother, who had already settled in Steubenville. She landed at Ellis Island unable to speak a word of English, searching for the train that would bring her to her brother. I can't imagine how frightened she must have been in this strange and vast country, and how sad she must have been to leave her family back in Poland.

My children were blessed that my Babka lived to the ripe old age of ninety-eight. I convinced her at one point to sit down with the kids to tell them about her life in Poland. Each of us tried to place ourselves in her shoes and wondered how we would have responded to those atrocities. Her story had a profound impact on our family, and it answered the question that I always had about her air of gentleness and peace: she had total faith in Jesus, and the Blessed Mother was her shield of protection.

## An Alcoholic Culture

I have many fond memories of childhood. I never thought much about the fact that we didn't have many material things—I really didn't know the difference. I can still visualize my parents spreading out the monthly bills on the kitchen table and placing down cash on each one to see if they had enough money to cover them all. All I know is that we had food on the table and that our parents loved my brother and me—even though they never verbalized it to us.

Neither of my parents was very emotionally expressive. My mother's father left the family when she was a little girl, and although she did experience some closure at the end of his life, she was just never comfortable speaking about her emotions. When she was dying, though, she gave me and my brother a wonderful gift: she told us, for maybe the first time, that she loved us very much. We knew that she did, of course, but it was so beautiful to hear her say it.

My father was raised in a tough home of Polish immigrants, and expressions of love were just not part of his personality. He had never experienced outward paternal affection, so how could he show it to us? In my adulthood, though, I began to greet my parents and my brother with a kiss. When I was raising children of my own, I made up my mind that I would tell them all the time that I love them. And I do the same with my grandchildren.

While expressions of love were hard to come by in our home, alcohol was not. When we lived in my great-grandfather's house, he would call my brother and me upstairs to give us money to run to the store and get him a pint of booze. He would pay us with candy that he had stashed in a nearby drawer while telling us not to tell our grandma or our mother. But he made one mistake: he gave away the location of the candy! So, when he would fall asleep in his rocking chair after hitting the bottle, Joe and I would pull off the candy heist. Eventually he caught on, though, and one day when we were grabbing the candy, he scared us half to death by yelling and throwing his cane at us.

Most family and community events, including those wonderful Sunday picnics, included a great deal of alcohol. The line between being fun and loose on the one hand, and having a problem on the other, was not always easy to discern. Both my parents were heavy drinkers, which created turmoil in their marriage and caused my brother and me some grief.

It is probable that one or both of my parents were alcoholics. The nature of family life went in cycles along with my parents' drinking. When they let themselves go, there were arguments; when they laid off the bottle, there was peace. It demonstrates the hold alcoholism can have on you that, while I could see and understand the connection between alcohol and family turmoil as a young man, I fell into those same cycles of alcohol-based turmoil and peace later in life. (I was fortunate, I think, that my busy sports schedule kept me from getting too involved with alcohol in high school.)

There was a particular incident that caused the entire family much grief but ended up, in the long run, having a positive effect on things around our house. My dad came home one evening, and we knew he had been drinking whiskey because whiskey made him mean. My brother and I were upstairs in our room studying when he came in and started wrestling with us. We weren't interested because he was clearly not in control. He got rougher with me and placed me in a headlock, which I finally escaped from, but I was mad because it had really hurt. So I threw a shoe at him, and he chased me. We had a very steep stairway that went down to the first floor. I ran down it, but my dad stumbled and fell, slamming his head against a door.

For a moment we all thought he was dead, but he got up with his nose split wide open. Things calmed down quickly, and my mom put some towels on his bleeding nose. After he cleaned up, my dad and I drove to the hospital for stitches — with me holding the towel over his nose. The next morning my dad apologized to us all for his behavior, and I never remember him drinking whiskey from that day on.

The good far outweighed the bad in our family. But I can't help but look back on my childhood and see foreshadowing of my later problems with alcohol.

## Cultural Catholicism

I can't remember my family ever talking about our Faith (and certainly not a personal relationship with Jesus Christ) even though we were very close. But like nearly everyone else in Steubenville, we had a crucifix on the wall and a statue of the Blessed Mother on the table, and my parents saw to it that we attended Catholic schools and attended Mass every Sunday. I simply took my Faith for granted; I never questioned or doubted it.

The Dominican nuns in grade school would drill the Faith into us by making us memorize the *Baltimore*. We had four or five priests always stationed at St. Peter's, and they would administer the sacraments to us while also helping with counseling and discipline. We always had special school Masses, Stations of the Cross, and basic Marian devotions such as a May Crowning. As an altar boy I had to learn all of the prayers and responses in Latin.

Despite all of this, my prayer life was almost nonexistent because I really was never taught at home, church, or school about the importance of having a personal relationship with Jesus and establishing a personal prayer life. The practice of our Faith was a habit, not a relationship with Christ. More than that, it was a habit we often didn't understand—especially because Mass was in a language we didn't understand.

On top of this, it was an expectation, even in Catholic Steubenville, that we didn't talk about Faith outside the church. Religion and politics: These were the two things you weren't supposed to bring up with other people. As my parents didn't share their feelings with us, it was very rare for people to share their faith journey with others. But, as I would later learn, faith *needs* to be shared in community to be truly alive.

Even though the Church was at the center of our lives—school, activities, and, of course, Mass were all "Catholic"—a living faith was not.

## Friday Night Lights

The towns of the Ohio valley between East Liverpool, Ohio, in the north and Wheeling, West Virginia, in the south were all cast from the same mold. Every town is anchored by a steel mill, a football stadium, a church, and a school. I'll let you guess the order of importance. In the fall, the local high school football game was the highlight of the week; most of the community would come out to support the team.

From one of my earliest Christmases, when I received my first football and baseball equipment, sports was number one in my life. When I was a kid everyone told me that my dad was a good athlete, and my younger brother was also talented, especially as a pitcher. Almost all of my uncles and male cousins played sports; in fact, my cousin Tom "Knute" Franckhauser played college football at Purdue and went on to play several years in the NFL for the Vikings and the Cowboys.

I really believe that what helped me improve as an athlete was not only the time my dad spent playing with me and encouraging me in the backyard, but also the activities my friends and I would dream up in our free time. We played whiffle ball in the street; we bounced a rubber ball against a concrete wall; we played slow-motion football in the mud; we made up games on the basketball court. I even practiced dodging leaves on the ground as I walked or jogged home from school. All of these things we were able to do just by being outside — not slouched in front of a television — and they naturally developed our athletic skills.

My baseball, football, and basketball careers began in the sixth grade at St. Peter's. I wasn't very big, so I played running back and defensive back in football, guard in basketball, and pitcher and outfielder in baseball. This continued during my first two years at Catholic Central High School. Going into my junior year, though, my cousin Tom, whom I idolized, suggested that my relatively small size made me better suited to being a wide receiver. This turned out to be a natural fit, because God had blessed me with hands that seemed almost to stick to the football. This was the move that allowed me to have the career that I did. Thanks, Tom!

While I played all three sports through high school, over time it became clear that my passion was for football and baseball.

*Abramowicz Family Christmas* (left to right): Babka;
my father, "Paper"; me; my great-grandmother
Kelly; my brother, Joe; my mother, "Dot."

*Striking a pose*: Official photo
from my senior year at Xavier
University (1966).

*Dapper*: With my beautiful bride, my Babka, and a family friend at the Polish Club of Steubenville.

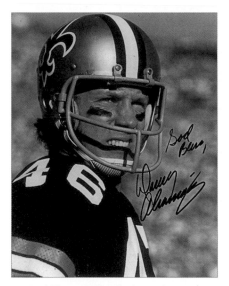

*God bless*: Official photo from my early years playing in New Orleans.

*Early-'70s hair*: On the town with
Archie Manning during the years we
spent together in New Orleans.

*Chicago Winter*: Coaching the Bears' special
teams on a cold day in Chicago.

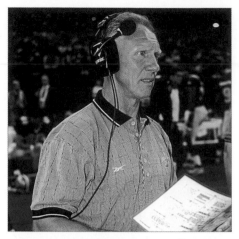

*Concerned*: Calling plays as offensive coordinator in New Orleans.

*Iron Mike*: Observing practice with my friend Mike Ditka.

*Paper and Pepper*: My father (left) and Claudia's
father (right) with Buds and a birthday cake.

*A real saint*: Holding the hand of the Holy Father
during my visit to the Vatican in 2004.

*Mons. Stanislaw Dziwisz*
*Arcivescovo titolare di San Leone*

From the Vatican, 8 October 2004

Dear Mr. Abramowicz,

The Holy Father and I thank you for your letter of August 2, 2004, the enclosed photos and the two autographed books, *Spiritual Workout of a Former Saint*.

Your journey through life has been memorable and challenging in all ways and we are sure it will touch many hearts and minds. Should your continued journey through life bring you to Rome, please call ▮▮▮▮▮▮ to see what can be arranged for you to meet the Holy Father.

We remember your cousin, Bishop Alfred, of blessed memory, prayerfully. May he rest in peace.

We pray, also for you and those you love. May this chapter in your life be spiritually rewarding and hope-filled, knowing God's bountiful and merciful love.

May these beautiful autumn days be a reminder of the great beauty that awaits us.

Sincerely yours in Christ,

✠ Stanislaw Dziwisz

Danny Abramowicz
909 Poydras Street
Suite 1700
New Orleans, Louisiana 70112
U.S.A.

*The letter*: The special note from the Pope's righthand man that led to our meeting.

*Papal pilgrimage*: Posing with Claudia in front
of a statue of Pope St. John Paul II in Poland.

*Make way for Coach Danny*: Keeping my
balance during a trip to the Holy Land.

*Chip off the old block*:
Playing my favorite game
with my grandson Ward.

*Family*: With Claudia and three of my
grandsons: Dillon (top right), Johnathan
(bottom right), and Anthony (bottom left).

I was always playing a sport, even during the summer, when I played in a summer baseball league. Thank goodness for that baseball league; looking back, I think my busy schedule during downtime from school kept me out of a lot of trouble.

This was before the near professionalization of high school sports that we have today; we weren't being groomed for pro sports as teenagers. Sure, it was competitive—very competitive! High school sports were the big game in town! But it was always more about representing our school and our town—as athletes and as young men—than about preparing for the next level.

Through those high school years, though, I was developing skills under some great coaches who were tough but fair with us rowdy boys. To this day, when I'm asked who my favorite coach in my career was, I say Ang Vaccaro, my summer American Legion baseball coach. Sure, he let me have it sometimes, such as when I tried to tag up to third on a short fly ball to left field—but I deserved it! My coaches made me a better person.

As much as I loved baseball, though, football was always at the top of my list. We had a strong football team for my senior season at Catholic Central, and we won eight of ten games. Unfortunately, our two losses were against our biggest rivals. We lost to Niles McKinley, from up the road in Youngstown, 6-0—but I still think they got a little help from the local referees! Niles went on to win the state championship.

Even more memorable, though, was our last game of the year: a mud battle against our down-the-street rivals, the Steubenville Big Red. Due to the conditions, neither team threw a single pass during the entire game! Somehow both teams scored some points, but we were on the losing end, 20-6. Even though our year ended on a sour note, it had been the best season in my four years at Catholic Central.

During that year there weren't many college coaches knocking on my door, probably because I was a 5-foot-11, 155-pound slow receiver. But I had a good set of hands and had put up strong numbers for a strong program. I didn't know what to expect. As much as I respected my father's work ethic, I didn't want to do the backbreaking work he and my friends' dads did for the rest of my life. But if I didn't get a scholarship, I wasn't going to college.

There was one coach who saw something in me: Ed Biles from Xavier University in Cincinnati. I am fairly sure that John King Musio, our bishop in Steubenville, who was from Cincinnati and had many ties to Xavier, had some influence on Coach Biles's decision to offer me and another teammate full-ride football scholarships.

I'll never forget when, on my official visit, Coach Biles asked me if I needed to go home and discuss the school's offer with my parents. I immediately replied, "I have already thought it over, and I accept your offer." There was no discussion needed—this was my chance. I thanked him and told him that I would not let him down.

## A Rocky Start

During the summer before my first year at Xavier University, my plate was pretty full. I played American Legion baseball, worked out strenuously to prepare for my freshman year of football, and had a job at the City of Steubenville Maintenance Department. I remembered the promise I made to Coach Biles that I would not let him down, so when I reported to the Xavier Fieldhouse in August to attend our first meeting, I was scared and nervous —but I felt prepared. I recognized that I was presented with a great opportunity, and it was up to me to take advantage of it. Meeting players from all over the country did make me a bit anxious, although once we hit the practice field with full pads and I got knocked on my butt—and then knocked someone else on his—things were fine.

The biggest game for our freshman team (NCAA rules didn't allow freshman to play varsity football at the time) was an away game against the University of Kentucky. They were highly favored, but we looked forward to the challenge. Late in the game, we were down 14–0 and had the ball on our own 35-yard line. The coach signaled me to punt on fourth down (we didn't have a specialist punter on the freshman team). But as we broke the huddle, I grabbed Dick Eroshevich, my high school teammate, and whispered to him to run a shallow pass pattern. I would fake the punt and throw to him for the first down. He looked at me as if I were crazy because he knew that the coach, who was a retired marine, would kill us both if this failed.

Everything seemed to be going well until Kentucky's NFL-bound lineman, "Mo" Moorman, stormed in, batted the pass in the air, and intercepted it. The only guy between 6-foot-5, 260-pound Mo and the goal line was 5-foot-11 me! I tried to tackle him, but I could grab only one of his legs, so he dragged me down the field until a few of my teammates came to my rescue and we tackled him.

As I trotted toward the sideline, I could see Coach, and his face was fire-engine red. I explained that I thought I could catch the defense off guard, but he wasn't hearing it. He then instructed some of the players to gather around us to block the vision of the spectators while he punched me in the gut a few times. I deserved it! After the game, which we lost, 21–7, he pulled me off to the side and said he was very proud of my competitive attitude, but I should never disobey him again. I didn't.

The academic life was a rude awakening for me. The university stressed its high academic standards, and they expected every student—yes, even the athletes!—to put academics at the top of his priority list. I remember getting my first reading assignment, which I figured needed to be completed in two weeks. But one of my classmates told me it was for the next class! I had never done that much reading in such a short period.

Many of the Jesuit priests who were my professors made themselves available to me for tutoring and counseling. Without this support, I'm not sure I would have graduated. The Jesuits were passionate about athletics, and so they were thrilled if I caught a few touchdown passes and helped the team succeed, but they were just as thrilled when I handed in my assignments.

Throughout that freshman year, I played not only football, but baseball and even some basketball. My first-semester grades were good enough to allow me to participate in spring sports, but my many responsibilities—not to mention partying—were becoming overwhelming. In the back of my mind I began to wonder if I was cut out for college life.

## Summer of Steel

At the end of the school year, I was really ready to go home and get some rest. Shortly after returning to Steubenville, I sat down with my parents to discuss my first year in college. I mentioned that I was beginning to wonder whether college was the right choice for me. After our short conversation, my dad didn't have much to say, and he hurriedly left the house.

Later that day he returned and dropped a pair of steel-toed work boots in front of me. He said he had found me a nice summer job: I was to report to the blast-furnace department of Wheeling Steel Corporation at 7:00 the next morning and ask for a man called Alabama. And that was that. As I got ready for bed that night, I told myself that I'd prove to my dad that I could handle the steel mill.

The following morning I reported to the front gate of Wheeling Steel. I stepped into a dirty, dimly lit room with a group of workers already sitting on benches awaiting their assignment for the day. Some guys I knew from high school greeted me with a friendly taunt: "Here comes the college boy." A few minutes later Alabama walked in and barked at me to grab a shovel and wheelbarrow and to follow him. There was no friendly orientation or welcome; it was straight to work.

He showed me how the molten steel comes out of the blast furnace and down a set of troughs, then pours into a ladle car on a track below the floor of the blast furnace. Alabama finished his little presentation, and we continued down the steps to the huge ladle car, which was parked in a dark lower level. He explained that my job would be to clean the spills off the track. I had to use a pick to loosen the slag steel before it hardened, then shovel the loose pieces into the wheelbarrow and haul them down the tunnel to a dump area.

That first day was a hard lesson about what it's really like to work in a steel mill. After about a month I had worked several assignments—none of which I liked. I wondered if I could possibly do this for the rest of my life.

Finally, one morning Alabama told me to follow him up to the floor of the blast furnace. I had never worked up there, so my heart was racing a bit. He told me to grab a wheelbarrow and a shovel, and he grabbed a huge crowbar. The night shift had emptied the furnaces and poured the steel into the ladle car, and some of the slag residue was left in the troughs. He took the large crowbar and stepped into the trough. He chipped away at the slag that had cooled and hardened, breaking it into small chunks and shoveling it into a wheelbarrow, which he then hauled down a narrow catwalk and dumped into the ladle below.

I watched him every step of the way, but I was distracted by the noise, the odor, and the incredible heat. That was the hardest, hottest, most dangerous job I ever had. All I could think about were the dangers of the mill and how my Uncle Walter had lost both of his legs in an accident there.

That evening after dinner I told my dad that I was definitely going back to Xavier and that he would never hear me complain about college again.

## Growing Athletically, Stunted Spiritually

Once I made up my mind that I wanted to stay in college, the remaining three years at Xavier were some of the most enjoyable of my life. During my sophomore year we held our own on the gridiron against stiff competition; I was excited to be the starting split end on offense and the starting defensive end.

Thank goodness that after my sophomore year, the NCAA changed the rules to allow for substitution, so I focused on my offensive role. During that year of going both ways, our other defensive end was 4 inches taller and 65 pounds heavier than I. Where do you think the other team liked to run the ball? I was totally beat down by the end of that season.

After the spring baseball season, my coach invited me to play in a summer league, which I happily accepted. That ended up being the end of my baseball career. Coach Biles insisted that I focus on the sport that was paying my tuition: football. After an injury-shortened summer playing baseball in Indiana, I hung up my bat and glove for good.

My junior year at Xavier was very productive on the football field as well as in the classroom. Our team went 8–2 under the leadership of our quarterback, Carroll Williams, one of the few black quarterbacks in college football in the mid-'60s. Carroll was a tremendous athlete and a dynamic leader; I was proud to be selected with him as a First Team Catholic All-American.

Academically, I was beginning to get the hang of things, and I didn't feel so overwhelmed. My grade-point average by the end of my junior year had stabilized thanks to the tutoring of the Jesuits and a little more organization and studying on my part.

Looking back on those years, I can see that even though I was succeeding academically and athletically, my spiritual life was regressing. I still attended Sunday Mass on campus, but that was about the extent of it. I had no prayer life; my faith was little more than an extension of my childhood faith. I went through the motions, but I didn't understand why. More importantly, I didn't feel the presence of Jesus in my life.

I fell into a pattern of partying, which led to heavy drinking. I indulged all the temptations one would expect a college football player to be faced with. Darkness was slipping into my life, and the light of faith was diminishing. College seems to be the prime time in young people's lives when they begin to drift away from their faith, or even leave it altogether. I can't remember any ministry on Xavier's campus that reached out to students who were struggling with their faith. If there was such an organization, it never reached out to me.

Currently there are a number of college campuses with Catholic Newman Centers, whose mission is to support students and provide a place to practice their Faith. Curtis Martin, a close friend of mine, founded a ministry called Fellowship of Catholic University Students (FOCUS), which evangelizes students and trains them in the Catholic Faith so they can go on to evangelize other students. It is a wonderful and successful ministry. I only wish we had something like FOCUS when I attended college; it might have spared me so much of the grief that I faced later.

Despite these spiritual struggles, I returned to campus for my senior year feeling great about my life. That summer, I had gotten married.

## Young Love

But let's back up a little bit.

I had met Claudia DiPrinizo during my junior year of high school. Her cousin, Tony D'Andrea, was my best friend; I didn't know it at the time, but his casual introduction at a Christmas party ended up being the best thing that ever happened to me.

About a year later, our paths crossed again in the hallway at school. I recognized Claudia but didn't remember her name — but she caught my attention. Later that day, I got her phone number from Tony, and I called her that night. After a lengthy conversation, I asked her out on a date to a movie. We went to see *The Birds*, which scared the daylights out of both of us. I was surprised that she wanted to keep seeing me after that! Even though I was a senior and she was a sophomore, we started dating on a regular basis for the remainder of my senior year and into college.

After my experience at the steel mill after my freshman year, I spent much of the rest of the summer with Claudia. About a week before I was to go back to school, though, she told me that she wanted to be free to enjoy her senior year of high school and that she no longer want to date me. I tried to convince her to change her mind, but to no avail; I walked home that night crushed.

A day or so later, Claudia called and asked me to come over to her house. Of course, I hung up the phone and immediately sprinted the three miles to her Italian neighborhood. She was waiting for me on the porch and told me that her mother had come to my defense! By the next summer, when she graduated from high school, we were officially going steady.

Shortly after returning home for Christmas break during my junior year, I went to Claudia's house for dinner. As I walked home, I realized how much I had really missed her during the semester. I knew that I was truly in love with her. That evening, as I lay awake in bed, I concluded that I'd better not let this woman get away from me. I knew we were very young, but we had been together for four years, and things were serious. I tossed and turned most of the night, trying to figure out how all of this could work out.

The next day I told my parents what I was planning to do, and even though they thought the world of Claudia, they weren't sure we were prepared for such a huge step. I prevailed on them, though, and told them I wanted to get married late in the summer, right before I went back for my senior year.

That evening, I was shaking all over as I made my way to Claudia's house. She asked what was the matter, and all I could say was, "Nothing, except that I want to marry you." And she accepted! Even so, she confessed that she was a little nervous about the whole thing. After all, she was only nineteen years old, and I was only twenty-one. But we both felt it was the right thing to do to press forward confidently and set a date for the end of the summer.

When I asked the DiPrinizos for their permission to marry their daughter, they were both glad for us while, naturally, expressing reservations about our youth. In the end, though, both families were much more happy than concerned. The only available date at Claudia's parish was Saturday, August 20 at 9 a.m. Beggars can't be choosers, so an early-morning wedding it was!

The rest of my junior year flew by quickly as I tried to keep my attention on academics and football. Some anxiety started setting in as I fully realized that I was about to be married. Was I ready for marriage? How would I support us?

Claudia, her mom, and her aunts were making all the plans for the wedding while I was away at school. During the summer, I worked for the city maintenance department to help save up some money, while Claudia worked as a secretary at the young Franciscan University of Steubenville.

A 9 a.m. wedding meant an early wake-up call, and for me and my buddies, it was a little difficult since we had my bachelor's party the night before at the Polish club. Although everyone made it to the church on time, I had seen better heads on cabbages than on the groomsmen! Immediately after the wedding Mass, we went to a church hall for breakfast, followed in the afternoon by a huge Italian feast. I think half of Steubenville was at the reception that evening; people just showed up, invited or not, and there was enough booze to float a battleship.

Claudia and I finally slipped out the back door of the reception hall to drive to our honeymoon destination in Pittsburgh. We were married in the second-dirtiest city in America and honeymooned in the dirtiest, but we were totally thrilled that all of the festivities were over and we were actually married! Suddenly, a car pulled up alongside us, honking its horn. It was not only one car, but a whole caravan of cars filled with our friends from the reception who decided to escort us to the Hilton Hotel in Pittsburgh!

## Back to Campus

After our honeymoon, I reported back to Xavier to begin football practice. Claudia and I lived in a small apartment complex near campus along with the other married members of our team. We all had a great time together that year, even though we didn't have two nickels to rub together.

Athletically, my senior year was mediocre—while I posted solid personal statistics, our 5–5 season was disappointing after the previous year's 8–2 record. The year was successful academically, though, which I attribute to marriage settling me down a bit. Claudia and I attended Mass at the campus chapel, but that was about the extent of our faith life. If some worrying situation arose and we thought we needed extra help, we said a Hail Mary or an Our Father, but that was that.

Xavier held its graduation ceremonies on a hot, sunny day in the football stadium. As the event was about to begin and things got quiet, a few of my buddies nudged me and said, "Is that your dad over there carrying an ice chest?" Lo and behold, I spotted my dad and my father-in-law lugging a huge cooler filled with beer into the stands; we could hear the bottles rattling together from all the way down on the field. As the ceremony continued, those two became the most popular people in the stadium, passing beers around the stands. What a memorable graduation day!

# CHAPTER 2

# ONE FOOT IN DARKNESS
# AND ONE IN THE LIGHT

Before graduation, I didn't know what was next. Xavier didn't have a big enough football program to attract professional scouts, so I was never contacted by an NFL team and had no expectation that I'd be drafted—even with seventeen draft rounds. I figured I'd just put my time as a football player behind me and go back to Steubenville to make a life for me and Claudia in our hometown, maybe by coaching at my old high school.

But one morning just before graduation, my dad called me to give me incredible news: I had been drafted in the seventeenth and final round by the expansion New Orleans Saints! I hadn't even been following the draft, but not just because I didn't expect to be drafted. Back then, there was no wall-to-wall television coverage of the NFL draft; it was just a low-key event in some hotel ballroom somewhere.

While I was incredibly excited to be joining an NFL team, my first impression of the Saints was not great. As I said, I found out I had been drafted from my dad—not from the actual team that picked me. In fact, the only communication I received from the Saints all summer was a letter inviting me to training camp, but they never made any arrangements for me. I actually negotiated my first contract with the staff of the Dallas Cowboys! They had volunteered to help the expansion Saints, who were still putting together the organization. That first contract was $17,000 for my first season, $18,500 for my second season, and a $3,000 signing bonus—the most money we'd ever seen.

When I reported to training camp in San Diego, Tom Fears, the head coach, apologized to me for the new team's incompetence. After we had a short meeting, I shook his hand and told him that all I wanted was a fair chance, and he agreed.

## A Fair Chance

Naturally, I was nervous as training camp began, but I knew in my heart that I was prepared physically and mentally. On the third day, they announced a special "man against man" drill. They lined up an offensive player next to the center and quarterback with a defensive player facing him. There was a ball carrier behind the offensive player, as well as a defensive back. The object was for the offensive player to block the defensive player at the snap of the ball, and for the ball carrier to avoid the defensive back. The drill was voluntary—first come, first served—although every player would eventually participate. I knew I had to do something extraordinary to catch the coaches' attention.

The first guy who volunteered on defense was a huge linebacker named, appropriately, Steve Stonebreaker. Even though I was shaking in my shoes, I jumped in there to face Stoney. It got very quiet. I told the quarterback and the center to go on a silent count and to snap the ball as soon as my hand touched the ground. It worked like a charm. I caught Stoney totally off guard and knocked him square on his rear end. Everyone cheered!

I started to walk away but Stoney grabbed me, turned me around, and said, "Rookie, you're not finished." I knew I was in trouble. We lined up, and as soon as my hand touched the ground, Stoney hit me with a forearm and knocked me for a flip. He stood over me and said, "Now we're even, Rookie." Everyone burst out laughing. I couldn't have scripted it any better. I was no longer just an unknown rookie: the episode caught the attention of the coaches and the veteran players.

In those days, the NFL played six exhibition games and fourteen regular season games. Halfway through the exhibition season, I had played only on special teams. Finally, one morning after breakfast I received the dreaded knock on my dorm-room door that meant that the head coach wanted to see me with my playbook in order to cut me.

I was totally surprised and disappointed because he had promised me a fair chance, but I hadn't played one down on offense. I went to Coach Fears' office, but I left my playbook in my room. Before he could say a word, I blurted out, "Coach, you didn't give me the fair chance that you promised, and I am not leaving." He was stunned and said, "You're totally serious!" I said, "Coach, I am as serious as a heart attack." There was a short silence that felt like an hour, and he looked me in the eye and said, "I will give you a chance in the next exhibition game; go get dressed for practice."

That Saturday we played the San Francisco 49ers in Portland, Oregon, and I started the game at wide receiver. I had never been so nervous in all my life, but I knew this would be my first and only opportunity to prove myself. And that's exactly what happened. I caught five or six passes in the first half alone, and I continued to play well on special teams. I had gotten my fair chance, and a few weeks later I made the final roster.

For the first seven games of the season, I played nothing but special teams, running down on kickoffs and crashing into wedges headfirst. At that pace I didn't know how long I would last in the league.

The eighth game of the year was a home game against the Pittsburgh Steelers—my childhood team. The starting receiver ahead of me had been injured the previous week, so I got the nod for the game. I was excited and really nervous, because I knew the game was going to be broadcast back in Steubenville, which is only twenty-five miles from Pittsburgh.

Just like that exhibition game against San Francisco, it went better than I could have hoped. I ended up catching 12 passes for 160 yards and a touchdown. For that effort, I earned the starting split-end position for the rest of my rookie season. In those seven games, I ended up catching 50 passes for 721 yards and 6 TDs, all team-leading figures. I was named to the All-Rookie Team and runner up to Mel Farr of the Detroit Lions for Offensive Rookie of the Year.

## Brush with Death

In the middle of that season my wife and I were blessed with our first child, a boy we named Danny Joe (DJ). Although it ended up being one of the most joyous days of our lives, it didn't begin that way. Claudia had a troubled pregnancy with preeclampsia, so she was bedridden off and on in the third trimester. Finally, in the middle of the night on November 13, 1967, she woke me up and informed me that her water had broken. I've never moved so fast in my life. I was more nervous than on the opening kickoff of the Saints' season. We arrived at the hospital, and early that morning our son was born.

Later in the day, while we were looking at our little boy through the window of the nursery, Claudia suddenly started to shake uncontrollably. She was immediately wheeled away, and people scurried around; they were very concerned. I was led to a private room where I anxiously awaited an update. My heart was racing, and I began to pray and cry. Shortly afterward, a doctor came in and informed me that my wife had gone into convulsions and that she was in the Intensive Care Unit, where they were trying to stabilize her. He told me to wait and to pray, as it could be a while.

I begged the Lord to let my wife live; it was the most—and most urgently—I had prayed in years, and maybe ever. After a few hours, the doctor came into the waiting room and informed me that Claudia was stable. I was incredibly relieved.

Just as in college, Claudia and I were practicing our Catholic Faith by going to Mass on Sundays, but we didn't have any kind of a prayer life. Once in a while we would go to Confession. You would think that this health scare would bring us closer to our Faith, but it didn't. We continued to do the bare minimum—just enough to keep our consciences clear.

## Starting

In my second year, I maintained my strong play, catching more passes for more yards than in my rookie season. It felt good to know that my rookie season was not a fluke, and my confidence was at an all-time high. But maybe the best story from that season happened (on the way) off the field.

Toward the end of the year, we were playing the New York Giants in Yankee Stadium, and a series of events during the game led to a massive brawl on the field, including fans! When I saw that even our biggest player was taking the worst of it, I made a beeline for our locker room in the dugout. But I forgot about the step down and smacked my head on the top of the dugout, which almost knocked me out, even with my helmet on.

As the players started to enter the locker room, I was sitting in a chair trying to gather my wits. Everyone asked me if I was all right, and I told them I had fought off two or three guys, but I was doing well. Later on during our plane flight home and after several beers, I embellished the story further.

Well, the next morning, all the players and the coaches were in the meeting room waiting for Coach Fears to address the team. It was awfully quiet after a tough loss. Coach entered the room and said that he had something very interesting to show us. When he turned on the game film from the previous day, it showed me slamming my head into the dugout! The place exploded in laughter — but I deserved it. I was never quite able to live that one down.

My third season in the NFL was my breakout year. I led the NFL in pass receptions, made First Team NFL All-Pro, and was voted the Saints' MVP by the players. The only incentive in my incentive-laden contract that I didn't achieve was the Pro Bowl clause. Our team offense ranked fourth in the entire NFL.

With all this success, my popularity increased among our fans, and I began receiving requests for speaking engagements and endorsements. All of this caused me to be away from home many evenings and nights, and my drinking increased. Meanwhile, Claudia and I were being introduced to important and fashionable people; we received invitations to dinner parties at the homes of some of the elite families of New Orleans.

The folks in New Orleans and around the Gulf Coast had been waiting for an NFL franchise for years. Now that they had one, they really embraced us. On the one hand, of course, it was wonderful. Who wouldn't love to be the talk of the town? It was like being the big man on campus, but the campus was an entire major city. We had the run of the place.

But all this notoriety also came with temptations. The only person more impressed with me than the fans was myself. Deep down inside I thought about my modest upbringing in Steubenville and said to myself, "Look at the incredible things I've accomplished. Boy, did I ever show them!" I let myself participate in the social life of the city to the fullest extent; drinking and partying was a way of life. (And this wasn't just any city; this was New Orleans!) After all, I felt as if I deserved it: I had made it to the NFL from Steubenville, so why not live it up?

Claudia and I went to Mardi Gras balls and other prestigious social events; I was even crowned king of one of the Mardi Gras parades—a huge honor in New Orleans. Although Claudia enjoyed most of this to a point, she certainly did not like my drinking. My behavior away from home was often inappropriate. Even though I hardly ever drank at home and I felt I was doing things the right way as a husband and father, the dual life was beginning to take its toll on all of us.

I convinced myself that since I was providing financially for my family and spending a little quality time with the kids, I was doing enough. Additionally, I had convinced myself that since I felt I was doing my family duties just fine, I could indulge in all the pleasures of being an NFL star "on the side." What I realize now, of course, is that you can't just dabble in sin. You can't be a doting father three nights a week and a party animal four nights a week and act as if they cancel each other out.

As I look back at that time of my life, I can see clearly that I had one foot in the dark and one in the light, but you're always going one way or the other. And I was sliding toward the dark.

## Ending

I continued to perform on the field at a high level even though we had one losing season after another. In 1971 the Saints drafted Archie Manning from Ole Miss in the first round, hoping he would turn the team around. Archie is a wonderful person and a great athlete, but he kept getting sacked and we kept losing. Finally, in 1973 after the opening game in which our rivals, the Atlanta Falcons, beat us 61-14, I asked the Saints to trade me. They did so the very next day, and I was off to the San Francisco 49ers. I loved New Orleans, but I just couldn't take losing any longer.

The 49ers had been a good team for many years, but the core of their team was beginning to age. Halfway through the season I injured my knee; before each game until the season ended, they shot Novocain into my knee and taped it up. A rash of injuries began to pile up, including to our starting quarterback, John Brodie, and my production dropped off. (We had to rely on backup quarterback Steve Spurrier, who had won the Heisman Trophy in college but never really flourished in the NFL.) We finished, again, with a losing season.

Before I returned to New Orleans after the season, I had a checkup with the 49ers' team doctor, who informed me that I would need a knee operation, and that it was team policy for players to be operated on by the team doctor. So after a short stay at home with my family, I flew back to San Francisco for the knee operation. When they opened my knee up, they found not only damaged cartilage but also many pieces of cartilage lodged behind my kneecaps, which had caused the pain during the season. I was never the same player after that operation. I lost a step of speed — speed I never had in the first place!

After one more season in San Francisco in 1974, my eighth straight season of losing, I had had enough; it was time to retire. I went home and told Claudia my decision, and she was very happy to hear the news. I think she thought this might finally settle me down by allowing me to focus more on my family and less on my drinking buddies and other social "responsibilities." After taking a break to rest my body and spend time with my family, I was offered a nice sales position with a trucking company. And life was briefly pretty normal.

Then, early one morning in October, I got a phone call from Bob Shaw, my first receivers coach with the Saints, who now worked on the Buffalo Bills' staff. He informed me that their number-one receiver was injured, and they wanted to sign me to serve as the backup to their rookie wide-out. I would be in-surance in case the kid didn't work out. The Buffalo Bills had enough talent to make it to the Super Bowl, so after all those losing seasons, the offer was very tempting. Claudia didn't want me to go, but she knew that I really wanted to give it a shot, so she agreed to it. The next day, I was on a plane headed to Buffalo.

In my first two games with the Bills, I didn't get my uniform dirty. From the very beginning, I didn't have a good feeling about the situation. The Bills' stadium and practice facility were outside Buffalo in an undeveloped suburb, and I was sharing a two-bedroom suite at a small motel. But I also missed my family. The third week I was there, I made up my mind to go home and hang up my cleats for good. My decision was confirmed when I opened the door to find a few inches of snow on the ground. I called my wife, and she told me it was sunny and 80 degrees in Louisiana. I told her I would be home that night!

My NFL career was finally over after eight years—not bad for a seventeenth-round draft pick from Steubenville! By worldly standards everyone could look at me and see a successful man. I had established an NFL record by making a reception in 105 games in a row, led the NFL in receiving in 1969, made All-Pro, and held all the Saints' career receiving records. More than that, I had a big house, nice cars, and a wonderful family. To an outside observer, my life was perfect.

# CHAPTER 3

# LORD, PLEASE HELP ME!

Despite all the wonderful things going on in my life, my spiritual life was not in order. Those eight years in the NFL were focused on building up my career, my family, and my social stature. I had plunged into the New Orleans social scene, going out multiple days per week to drink and, just as importantly, to keep up appearances. I would always make up some kind of excuse, sometimes partly true, sometimes totally untrue, to justify going out. All the while, the practice of my Faith was taking a backseat.

I got caught up in all the glamour. My only real faith was in all the press clippings about me and the people who flattered me because I was famous. I was totally caught up in the world.

But at the same time I really and truly loved my wife and kids. I never dreamed of doing anything to hurt them, but I had convinced myself that my selfish lifestyle didn't affect them. I was living in a dreamland of my own making. And this is how the devil traps us.

## Rock Bottom

After retiring from football, I thought that my NFL success would also ensure success after football. It seemed beneficial for my career to remain connected to the Saints and the NFL, so I accepted a radio-broadcast job as a color analyst for the team's radio broadcasts. It was tough to remain positive through five more years of losing Saints teams. Once, after a blowout loss against the lowly Tampa Bay Buccaneers, in order to save the players the embarrassment of post-game interviews I pulled the plug in the locker room that connected me to the broadcast booth. Management wasn't happy, but the players certainly were — and so was I.

My five years behind the microphone were just as tumultuous for me as they were for the Saints. I never realized how much I would miss the thrill of playing in the NFL, not to mention the fellowship of my teammates. I just couldn't settle on a day job that satisfied me. I tried several executive sales positions that didn't pan out. The expense accounts that came with those jobs were not good for me, as they enabled more excessive drinking. In fact, on occasion I would even drink in the broadcast booth, especially at halftime. The drinking caused mood swings that contributed to my job dissatisfaction, and all of these things together caused great strain on my marriage.

Many times over the years, from my playing days into these dark years, I told Claudia I was sorry for my behavior and moodiness, and I promised that I would turn over a new leaf. Each time I would be better for a few weeks and then fall back into the same old patterns. All this left me feeling depressed, which made things worse for everybody.

Although I knew Claudia never *wanted* to leave me, she was at the end of her rope. She always held out hope that I would permanently change, but that hope was running out. If it weren't for our three children, I really believe our marriage might have ended.

To make things worse, radio-station management issues brought an end to my radio career. One of the last anchors in my life was gone. Through all this turmoil, as long as I wasn't drinking, my relationship with my family was very good. I rarely drank in the house, and I wasn't an angry drunk. But I didn't know how to hold on to the good times without falling right back into the bottle. I was a lost ball in high weeds.

Finally, I woke up on December 15, 1981, with another hangover, but I could tell something was different. I rolled over in bed, looked at my beautiful wife, then got up and peeked into the rooms of our three sleeping children. I went into the bathroom to shave, and for the first time I *really* looked into the mirror — into my eyes and down into my soul. And I hated what I saw. There was nothing but darkness. I saw a drunk, a liar, a phony — everything that I didn't like in others is what I saw in myself. I was disgusted with myself and saw no value in the life I was leading.

These were the thoughts of an ex-NFL star who everyone thought had his act together. I knew that I needed help; I was at the bottom of the barrel. And so I cried out: "O Lord, please help me!"

## "Grateful Alcoholic"

When we are desperate and cry out for help from the Lord, He is always there in His divine mercy and love to answer our prayer. As soon as I calmed down, I knew the Holy Spirit was putting the thought into my head to call Fr. Tom Cronin, a Jesuit priest and a friend. I told him that I needed to see him about a personal issue, and he suggested the next morning, but I insisted that it had to be right away. I went over immediately and told Fr. Tom that I had a real problem with alcohol that was ruining my life and my marriage. He grabbed my arm, looked at me intently, and told me that I had come to the right place: he, too, was an alcoholic.

He told me about a friend of his named Buzzy who had helped him through his struggles with drinking. The next thing I knew, I was heading over to Buzzy's office. Although I was pretty nervous when we first sat down to talk, I soon felt comfortable talking with him. Buzzy asked me to fill out a short questionnaire to help determine the extent of my problem. After looking over the results, he told me my problem was serious. He looked me dead in the eyes and said, "Danny do you want help?" As tears welled up in my eyes, I said firmly, "Yes." I agreed to attend an Alcoholics Anonymous meeting with him that very night. As I headed to my car, I was overcome with a fear that I wouldn't be able to beat this addiction.

Driving home I went over the series of events that had trans-pired that day—from waking up and knowing that something was different, all the way to agreeing to attend an AA meeting with a person I had just met. The only way I could make sense of it all was to believe that God's hand was upon me. When I got home I immediately sat down with my wife and explained what had happened. She was amazed and relieved that I was finally doing something about my drinking problem—something more than empty promises. I asked her to pray for me, and she told me, beautifully, that she had been for quite some time.

I ended up bringing my brother, Joe, who also struggled with drinking, to the AA meetings with me. The first meeting was uncomfortable, but it was helpful to have my brother and my new friend there with me. Buzzy called me a few days after that first meeting to invite me to lunch, where he shared his story with me. As we were leaving, he turned to me and said that someday

I would be a "grateful alcoholic." As you can imagine, I looked at him as if he were nuts.

After several weeks of attending the meetings, I was working through the program pretty well, but I was not being totally honest with myself. Around this time, I was sitting in a meeting and the devil started to work on my mind: "You're not like the rest of these drunks. You haven't had a drink in three months. You could probably have a beer and it wouldn't even bother you. Why do you need to waste your time with this program?"

I stood up and headed for the front door to leave the meeting, when all of a sudden a lady in a wheelchair spoke: "I want to apologize to everyone for letting you down." By now I was at the front door and had grabbed the handle to leave. She continued, telling us how she had one drink that weekend after *fourteen and a half years* of sobriety, but one led to another and another, and she ended up being smashed all weekend. The scary part, she said, was that once she took that first drink, it was as if she had never stopped drinking. When she finished her story, I immediately went back to my seat, shaking. When the meeting ended, I stayed and cleaned up all the trash, which I had never done before.

As I drove home, I realized that I had not been entirely truthful in those previous meetings. Whenever I introduced myself by saying, "Hi, I'm Danny, and I am an alcoholic," I didn't really believe it. I was attending these meetings to please my wife, but I wasn't facing the fact that I was an alcoholic. At the very next meeting, I was the first person to speak up and when I said, "Hi, I'm Danny, and *I am an alcoholic*," I meant it from the bottom of my heart. From that day forward, I never looked back. My brother and I have been in the AA program for over thirty years, and after all of these years, I truly am a grateful alcoholic, just as

Buzzy told me I would be. God bless Buzzy and Fr. Tom as their souls rest in peace.

## Settling Down

During my years of drinking, I made some poor financial decisions that were now coming back to haunt us. (This is what happens when you have "stinking thinking" from drinking.) Although I managed to get off the hook for two particularly bad invest-ments, we were still almost totally broke. I remember sitting in our backyard with anxieties racing through my mind about the sale of our house, how all the proceeds would have to go to the bank, and how we would be left with $500 to our name. And to top it off, I hated my job in the insurance business. I realized that I had put my family in a real bind, with no obvious way out of the mess. I began to cry, asking God for help. At that moment, Claudia walked up to me and saw me crying. She comforted me, as she has done many times in our marriage, and assured me: "The Lord will provide."

The next day, I got a call from one of my insurance clients—the head of an oil service company. He wanted to give me a job—not just any job, but a position that would pay more money and offer better benefits than my insurance work. He even of-fered to advance me one month's pay! I was so stunned that I couldn't speak. Once I could speak again, I quickly accepted and told Claudia. We both laughed with joy at how quickly the Lord had worked!

My life finally began to settle down: I had a job I liked; my debt problems were under control; and I was attending AA meet-ings regularly. We still attended Mass as a family every Sunday, and my wife was praying more, but I still prayed only when troubles arose. I did start to sense, however, that the Lord was encouraging me to go deeper in my faith.

## A Personal Charismatic Renewal

One morning I was in the backyard having my coffee and reading the sports page; once again I could sense that the Lord was stirring my spirit. A few minutes later, a strong gust of wind came and blew my newspaper all over the yard. As I began to pick it up, I noticed a small ad for a Catholic Bible study at a parish in the inner city of New Orleans. Something inside me told me to sign up for it. So I nonchalantly went into the house, picked up the phone, and reserved a space.

I didn't tell Claudia about it because I didn't want to let her down again if I couldn't follow through. And if I did follow through, I wanted to be able to surprise her!

The following week I attended my first class. There were about twenty people in attendance — mostly women except for me and an older man. I wondered what in the world I was doing there. I had purchased a Catholic Bible just before the meeting. The instructor, a man named Benny Suhor, began with a prayer and then asked us to open our Bibles. It was very quiet in the room, and when I opened my brand-new Bible, it made a loud cracking sound. Everyone's heads turned, and I told them (falsely, of course) that I had this new one because I'd worn out my other Bible.

I thoroughly enjoyed the course, even though I didn't say much. Benny stopped me after the third or fourth class and invited me to a special prayer meeting that he attended on Wednesday nights at another local church. He was so nice and gentle that I couldn't turn him down, even though I really did not want to go. When I got home, I told my wife what had happened, and all she did was smile faintly. She knew what was happening to me.

As I was driving over to the prayer meeting, I reassured myself that if I didn't like the event, I'd just sneak out the back door. But the church ended up being so packed that I was squeezed into a pew, and my escape plan went out the window. Suddenly the music started up, but this wasn't the typical church choir that I was used to; these people had instruments, and they were singing songs I had never heard before. In fact, I had to look at the crucifix to make sure I was in a Catholic church!

I must say, on one hand I felt uncomfortable, but on the other hand, I sort of liked it. While I wasn't a fan of the waving arms in the air, I loved that they were praising and worshipping the Lord. Once they stopped singing, things got quiet for just a second, and then all of a sudden it sounded like a swarm of bumblebees. Everyone had their arms up in the air and started speaking "words" that I couldn't understand. All I wanted to do was to get the heck out of that place, but I was blocked in. I looked around, though, and noticed that almost everyone had their eyes closed and had smiles on their face. They were praising the Lord, and I was in the back of the church with a frown on my face. I said to myself: "I want what they got."

Although I enjoyed the prayer meeting, I still couldn't get out of there fast enough. As I turned the corner and headed to my car, much to my surprise, there was Benny waiting for me. He was the last person I wanted to see. He invited me to attend a seven-week course called the *Life in the Spirit Seminar* starting that next week prior to the prayer meeting. Immediately, and without thinking, I said yes. Driving home, I wondered what in the world was going on.

Over the next several weeks, I regularly attended a Bible-study course, a *Life in the Spirit Seminar*, and a Catholic charismatic prayer meeting. I couldn't believe what was happening to me in such a short period; the Lord was working overtime on me!

The sixth week of the *Life in the Spirit Seminar* totally changed the course of my life. The instructor drew three circles on the board. He then drew three crosses: one just outside the first circle, one just inside the second circle, and one right in the middle of the third circle. He explained that the circles represented all the people in the world, and the crosses represented Jesus Christ.

The first circle signified a person who does not have Jesus in his life at all and is focused on temporal things such as money, power, and so forth. I couldn't relate to the first circle because I did have the Lord in my life, at least a little bit. The second circle represented a person who has the Lord in his life but is focused on something else. I could totally relate to this example, because my life was focused on booze and my ego; my family, my job, and even my God all revolved around me. Finally, the third circle is a person who has Jesus Christ at the center of his life.

I was convicted. I knew, beyond a shadow of a doubt, that I had to make Jesus Christ the center of my life. I could hardly wait until next week's session when they would pray over all of us for a renewal of the Holy Spirit in our lives.

## Falling Over for the Spirit

Catholics receive the Holy Spirit in the sacraments of Baptism and Confirmation. Once we have received these sacraments, though, we often allow the graces they give us to lie dormant for years because we rarely call on the Spirit to supply us with the necessary graces to help us in our walk through life. The Baptism in the Holy Spirit session is intended to renew our souls as other brothers and sisters in Christ lay hands on us and pray for a deeper outpouring of the Holy Spirit.

When the others laid hands on me in prayer I didn't have any kind of earth-shattering experience — just a warming sensation all over my body. I quietly asked Jesus to be the center of my life. Some people did experience outward signs or gifts, such as tears of joy or praying in tongues, but mine was a gentle movement of the Holy Spirit within my soul. I had a total sense of inner peace.

Claudia had attended and completed the *Life in the Spirit Seminar* several weeks before I did. She shared her experience with me, which had encouraged me to give it a shot. After I completed the seminar, we both knew that God was moving powerfully in our lives, and that He was calling us to go deeper in our faith. Together we signed up to attend another seminar called *Growth in the Spirit.*

Over time, I had more and more experiences of the Spirit moving in my life. Claudia had received the gift of tongues when her group prayed over her at the Baptism in the Spirit, but I did not. In fact, I had no interest in it because I thought it was a bunch of hocus-pocus. Several weeks later, my wife and I were at the Wednesday-night prayer meeting, and I was inspired to open myself up to the gift of tongues. It was awkward at first, but after a while, I could tell that it was just a higher form of prayer — a new language the Holy Spirit had given to me to express in worship what was in the depths of my heart.

During the mid-1980s the Catholic Charismatic Renewal flourished in the New Orleans area, and so the movement sponsored an annual gathering called the Southern Regional Conference, for which Claudia and I volunteered. During one of the first conferences we attended, they asked if I would be a "catcher" for one of the prayer teams. My responsibility was to catch any person who fell down as a result of being prayed over by the prayer team and then gently lay the person on the floor. They called this falling-down experience "resting in the Spirit." I agreed to it even though I thought this "resting in the Spirit" business was a farce — just as I had thought that speaking in tongues was.

The first night of the conference, I was assigned to help a prayer team of two older women. The first person to ask for prayer was so big that he could have been an offensive lineman. Not long after these two little old ladies started praying with him, he started swaying back and forth, and then he fell backward. I was in a perfect position to catch him, and I knew that he would just fall back gently into my arms, and I would ease him to the ground. But instead he fell back helplessly with all his weight! It caught me off guard, and it was a tremendous struggle for me to deposit him safely on the floor.

As the team kept praying over people and I kept catching them, it became clear to me that they were totally at rest when they fell. When we finished praying with everyone, I was completely worn out; meanwhile, there were peaceful people resting in the Spirit on the floor all around me.

I was about to go back to my seat when one of the women in my prayer team asked if they could pray with me. They asked me to extend my hands and close my eyes. When I opened my eyes, I was on the floor looking up at the lights in the conference hall, totally at peace. As I got up, I looked over at my wife, and she had a huge smile on her face. To this very day, whenever someone prays with me by the laying on of hands, I am very susceptible to resting in the Spirit.

## Taking the Lead

Over the next year, our faith blossomed. In fact, we started to go to church not only on Sundays for Mass and Wednesday nights for the prayer meeting, but also at other times during the week. As a result of our going to Mass more often and taking time for personal prayer, the Word of God started to come alive in my life.

During my prayer time one morning, I thought I heard the Lord tell me that He wanted me to start a men's prayer group at my house. Of course, I thought it was just my imagination, so I dropped it immediately and didn't give it much thought. About a week later, the same thought came up again, and I said under my breath, "Lord, maybe a card game, but not a prayer meeting." Once again, I just moved on. Once more it came back, and this time the Lord spoke to my heart loud and clear: "I want you to start that prayer group—now!" I had never experienced anything like it; it shook me up a bit because the message was so clear.

The next morning, I called Buzzy, who was not only my Alcoholics Anonymous sponsor but also my spiritual director. He knew that I was confused and anxious over all of this, and so he assured me that this is how the Spirit often works, and he promised to help me. So I contacted Benny and some of the friends I had met at the Wednesday prayer meeting and at my parish. I invited twelve men—some I barely knew—to the first prayer meeting at my home. And they all showed up! God knew that I needed a new circle of friends; He just went about it in a very unusual manner.

When everyone showed up at the house that first night back in 1985, I really had no idea what I was doing. We basically just sat around getting acquainted, and toward the end of the evening, Buzzy suggested that we say some prayers. Everyone said that they would return, though, and one of the guys even offered to bring his guitar so we could sing a few songs. At the next meeting he led us in some praise songs, and a few guys shared some things that were going on in their lives. This ability to share struggles candidly became the foundation of the prayer group.

After six months, we had more than fifty men showing up at these prayer meetings, which we called Monday Night Disciples (MND). Over time we established a regular ninety-minute format: thirty minutes of praise and worship songs, fifty minutes of personal sharing and testimony, and ten minutes of concluding prayers. The men would then hang around for another hour or so, chatting and eating.

Sharing was becoming the main characteristic of our meetings. Our culture expects men to keep their troubles and feelings to themselves. We aren't supposed to lean on anybody for help and support because that would show weakness. But this isn't healthy for anyone—and certainly for anyone dealing with spiritual struggles.

Our small group provided a place where men could be totally honest about what was going on in their lives. On top of that, they found men who had gone through (or were going through) similar difficulties who could give them advice and support. Transparency is critical, because it allows us to bring out the true feelings that we have stored in our hearts—and then to learn from others. At the same time, transparency helps others in the group who may not yet be comfortable sharing their own hearts.

When you are involved with a group of Christian men who meet regularly, you can develop the types of close, brotherly relationships that just don't happen in secular society. It's critical, of course, that what is said in these meetings stay there. Gossip destroys the trust that is necessary to forming brotherly friendships.

The most harrowing story we heard in the MND group was from a man whose son was in prison for murder. The boy had been an excellent student and an all-star athlete but had secretly been abusing steroids. This addiction led to a psychological break, and he randomly broke into his neighbors' home and killed the couple living there. Needless to say, it was an incredibly emotional moment for the father to tell that story to our group. I hate to think what might have happened to him if he didn't have an outlet to share and to grieve. Blessedly, his son found Christ in prison, even leading a Bible study there.

The MND group grew to the point where our home could no longer hold it. We had to move furniture into the driveway just to fit everybody! So we moved the gathering to a local parish, and then, as growth continued, the group split into multiple smaller groups to facilitate sharing and discussion. Soon there were MND groups all around the New Orleans area.

I can't even begin to describe how much of a blessing MND has been to me and how much I love these men as brothers in Christ. Even though I currently live in Chicago, I stay in touch regularly with my brothers in New Orleans. If I would call them and ask them to come to Chicago to help me, they would be there without hesitation — and I would do the same for them. When God asked me to start this group, it was because He knew that I needed Christian brotherhood in order to fight the spiritual battles that were ahead of me. I am so humbled that God has used MND to provide that brotherhood for so many other men.

## Sharing My Testimony

Several years into my spiritual walk, I felt as if I was getting my life back in order. By this time the news about my conversion experience had begun to spread around the Catholic community, so I was receiving invitations from churches and AA groups to give my testimony. Up to this point, I had immediately turned down any requests to speak because I didn't feel that I was ready to share my story with anyone, except at regular AA meetings. I was still fragile, and I lacked the confidence to step out and give witness to what God had done in my life.

But now I had a sense that the Spirit was nudging me to share my story, so I began taking baby steps. I started by accepting some invitations from AA organizations, small prayer groups, and various parishes. Soon I was addressing that first Wednesday-night prayer meeting that started me on this path of conversion, and then the Southern Regional Conference in front of thousands of people.

As I continued to grow in my faith, I increased the time I spent in prayer. One evening I was sitting in the Adoration Chapel, and I heard the Lord calling me to concentrate my efforts on evangelizing Catholic men—it was as simple and clear as that. I just knew this was from the Holy Spirit, because He knew that I would be effective with men because of my background as an athlete—as long as I would continue to follow His way.

# CHAPTER 4

# COACH DANNY

My life had finally settled down. I had a good job, my family life was in order, and I was walking in the faith and evangelizing men through speaking and leading small groups, as the Lord had instructed me. I felt deep down inside, though, that the Lord had something more for me to do, but I wasn't sure what it was.

One day during prayer, the idea of coaching came back in my mind. I had often thought about coaching, but I would always let the idea drop. It never seemed to be realistic or the right time for it. But this time it was different. With the confidence that comes from the Spirit, I knew this could be a possibility. It was 1989, and I was forty-four years old—I wasn't sure if this was a good move, but I wanted to be obedient to the Lord. I intensified my prayer life, and Claudia and I focused our attention on discerning God's will.

Several days later, I picked up the newspaper and read that the head football coach at Jesuit High School in New Orleans had taken a coaching position at Tulane University. While I had initially thought the Lord might guide me to college or professional football, both of our boys had graduated from Jesuit, so I was very familiar with the school. That evening I went to the Adoration Chapel to continue my discernment, and the Lord put on my heart that Jesuit was the place where he wanted me to coach.

The very next day I contacted the president of the school, Fr. Philip Postel, to set up a meeting. He told me that they had already received more than twenty applications for the position, not including three from the current staff. Several days later, though, I met again with Fr. Postel and the athletic director for several hours. Less than a week later, I received a call from Father, offering me the job. And a week after that, I was coaching and teaching physical education at Jesuit High School.

Sometimes the Lord takes a long time to make something happen, and sometimes He works very quickly!

## Building a Team

My first year as head coach was very difficult. We ended up winning only three games; there was division within the coaching staff; the players lacked enthusiasm; and, to top it off, the quarterback was a spoiled brat. I knew I had to make some changes to the coaching staff, and the players needed an attitude adjustment in the off-season.

The first thing that I wanted to establish was that we were a team, not a bunch of individuals. I had the coaches remove all the locks from the lockers to indicate to them that if we couldn't trust one another, we would never succeed. I also wanted to bring our Faith into everything we did, so we hung crucifixes at both entrances to the locker room, and we concluded practice with team prayer. I could tell that some of the coaches and players weren't comfortable with this, but it was important to make the school's Catholic identity part of our team. We even began attending Mass as a team every so often, and we supported other school activities to show appreciation for the support we received from the school community.

During the summer, I announced to the players that we would go to a local college for a week of training camp before school began. They were totally excited about the idea of training camp—it sounded like the pros! I let them know that no parents would be permitted to attend any of the practices, but that we would have an open scrimmage on Saturday and a family picnic afterward.

The week in camp was grueling. We practiced early in the morning, and then again late in the afternoon in order to beat some of the heat. After each morning practice, we would take off our pads and, after prayer, the players would break into groups by position, go off to sit in a shady place, and share about their personal lives with one another. We didn't tell football stories; we just talked about what was going on in our lives—the good and the not so good. This was great for the kids because as coaches we were open and transparent, which helped the kids relax and open up. Of course, anything that was shared in these huddles stayed in there, as with Monday Night Disciples. At the close of the evening after our football meeting, we all gathered together as one big team, prayed for about fifteen minutes, and sometimes sang "Amazing Grace."

It was a bit difficult for the players (and some of the coaches) to get used to the idea of sharing in this way. But football is the ultimate team sport, and if you want to build a strong team, everyone—coaches and players—must know and trust one another at a deep level. Once that trust is established, you can make a commitment to lay it on the line for one another on the field. By the end of the week, everyone had bought into the team concept.

These sessions were very similar to the Monday Night Disciples group meetings. Although the men were younger, many of the issues were the same. And they all needed—as we all do—the kind of trusting friendships that can come only from sharing about what's going on beneath the surface of their lives. Many of the relationships we formed that week remain strong to this day.

At the end of the camp, the boys were all positive; many even predicted that we would go undefeated. I think the parents, too, noticed something different in their sons as a result of this time we spent together at training camp.

We opened our season the next week with a shutout victory, and it was the beginning of a dream season that none of us will ever forget. One game at a time, we knocked off opponents. All of our hard work and preparation was beginning to pay dividends, but I believe the biggest difference was that we were playing as a team and that we truly believed in each other. And more than that, we had centered our efforts on our faith.

Going into our last regular season game against rival Archbishop Shaw, we were 9–0. Our team had created much excitement around the school, and the local press had expanded its coverage of the games. A few local businessmen and Jesuit alumni even offered to put up the money to rent the Superdome to host this game, which is exactly what happened!

For most of the players on both teams, this would be a once-in-a-lifetime experience. We knew that we would have to play a flawless game, since Archbishop Shaw was a powerhouse boasting six or seven major college recruits. There were almost twenty-five thousand people in the dome, and as we approached the opening kickoff, excitement was in the air. Then our opponents fumbled on the first play of the game, and we recovered it and drove right down the field for a touchdown! It was the best opening we could have hoped for.

Unfortunately, that was the high point of the game for us. We were down 42–7 at halftime, and our locker room was like a morgue. One of our student team managers happened to pass by Archbishop Shaw's locker room and heard one of the coaches yelling to their players, "Let's see how high they can count!" When it was all said and done, we counted to 63. In the locker room after the game, I knew the guys were beaten down, but I told them to keep their heads up and stay focused, because the playoffs were around the corner.

What our team accomplished in the state playoffs after such a humiliating loss proved the character and fight in this group of young men. We went on to win three playoff games in a row against difficult opponents before losing in the state semifinals to an outstanding team from Catholic High of Baton Rouge, who were led by running back Warrick Dunn, who went on to be a three-time Pro Bowl selection in the NFL.

## Old Friends, New Opportunities

The following year we had an up-and-down season after graduating several starters. We just couldn't recapture the magic of that nearly undefeated season, but I still think the team environment helped the boys mature individually and as a group.

Near the end of the season, I received a phone call from the Chicago Bears asking if I would be available to lead their team chapel service before their upcoming game in New Orleans. Since we played most of our games on Saturday nights, due to the limited availability of the public stadium, we used, Sundays were very busy days for the coaching staff, but I felt as if the Spirit was nudging me to accept. After all, it would be a good opportunity to share my story with these NFL players.

I went to the hotel that morning, expecting to do the chapel service, go to Mass with my wife, and then return to my office for staff meetings. NFL chapel services are essentially a short non-denominational Bible study and sharing time. As I got settled in the room, much to my surprise, Coach Mike Ditka walked in.

Now, I had known Mike Ditka years ago during my playing days, and let's say he was one of the last people I thought I'd see at a chapel service. And he told me that I was one of the last people he'd expect to see leading a chapel service! Mike and I were both half-Polish guys from similar backgrounds: he was from the steel town of Aliquippa, just across the border from Steubenville in Pennsylvania. Over the years, we kept the friendship going, seeing one another at golf outings and speaking engagements.

After the service ended, Mike invited me to Mass and the pre-game meal with him. I tried to explain that I really needed to get back to the office, but Mike Ditka doesn't take no for an answer. So I relented, and we ended up really enjoying reminiscing about the old days and how both of us had changed our lifestyles. We had a lot in common, especially in how we had each rediscovered faith and in our conviction that the world needs more courageous men of faith—spiritual tough guys, not just physical tough guys—to stand up for what's right. He told me that he would be back in touch soon.

When both of our seasons had ended, Coach Ditka called me with a surprising offer: he wanted me to join the staff of the Chicago Bears as the special-teams coordinator. I was honored, but I told him that I was very happy coaching at the high school level because I could really have an impact on these young men's lives, both on and off the field. Of course, he wasn't about to let me off the hook that easily, so he asked me to fly to Chicago for a visit.

Claudia and I prayed over and discussed the matter, but neither of us was sure that the Lord wanted us to make this move. We decided, though, that I should at least make the trip to visit the Bears. I caught a flight to Chicago that day, met with Mike, and toured all of the facilities.

That evening I went to dinner with Mike and Diana Ditka and some of their friends. I happened to be sitting next to a gentleman who, in the process of our conversation, I discovered was the current special-teams coordinator! It was an incredibly awkward dinner; Mike had clearly not told him anything about a coaching change. The next morning, when Mike and I had breakfast, I told him that he was crazy for putting us in that position, but all he did was laugh. Iron Mike is one of the most honest and loyal guys I know, but he can also be a pain in the butt!

That very day, Mike offered me a two-year contract as the special-teams coordinator for the Chicago Bears, and a new chapter in my life began.

I was back home in New Orleans that night watching TV with my wife when the doorbell rang. Claudia answered the door, and much to her surprise, all the local TV stations were there with lights on and cameras ready! Apparently, the news broke on the wire service in Chicago that I had accepted the position with the Bears, and all the New Orleans stations announced it on the nightly news programs. I know this would create a very difficult situation for me with my players, because they would have wanted to hear it from me first—which is what I had intended.

First thing the next morning, I called for a team meeting, and when I walked in, I could see the boys were hurt and upset.

Finally, after a challenging two-hour meeting, the players seemed to understand, and they wished me luck. My three years at Jesuit were by far the most rewarding and fun-filled job I ever had. I will never forget my time there and the young men I was privileged to coach.

## Da Bears

My first season with the Bears, in 1992, had good times and not-so-good times. Coach Ditka knew the importance of special teams since he got his start as an NFL coach running special teams for the Dallas Cowboys under Tom Landry. So he gave me room to design my own playbook, sufficient practice time to implement my plan, and the ability to use starters to beef up the special teams.

During the off-season I studied what other teams were doing with their special teams, and I realized that most had very conservative approaches. In response, our special teams took on a more aggressive style, and we ended up blocking several punts, running some fake punts and field goals, and executing a few trick plays throughout the season.

The turning point in our season, and what I believe eventually led to Coach Ditka's firing, occurred in the fifth game. We had started the year strongly with a 3-1 record and were in Minnesota to play the Vikings. In the pre-game meeting Coach Ditka told quarterback Jim Harbaugh, now the head coach at the University of Michigan, not to change plays at the line of scrimmage under any circumstances due to the noise in the stadium. But in the fourth quarter, as we were up 20–0, that's exactly what he did. The resulting broken play resulted in an interception return for a touchdown; the Vikings then followed up with 14 more points, beating us 21–20. It was one of the worst losses I have ever experienced. After that game, our team fell apart, and we ended up having a losing season.

Toward the end of the season, rumors started flying that Coach Ditka's job could be in jeopardy. He didn't mention a word about it, so we assumed it was nothing more than a rumor. But a few days after the season ended, after all the players had checked out of the facility, Coach Ditka informed us that he had been fired. We all thought that Iron Mike deserved better.

The next morning, he came back to clear out his office, and as he was leaving, he stopped by my office with a cigar in his mouth (of course), and he dropped a piece of paper on my desk and said, "Thanks for your effort!" I looked down and saw a personal check in the amount of $10,000. If there's one thing you can always say about Mike Ditka, it's that he's a generous and loyal man.

With Coach Ditka gone, all the other coaches would have to reapply for their jobs or move on. During the next few days, Claudia and I spent quite a bit of time in prayer and discussion about our future. We just couldn't believe the Lord would have us move to Chicago to take this job, and then strand us here less than a year later. While my fellow coaches, mostly veteran NFL staffers, burned up the phone lines working their contacts around the league, I just kept going about my business in my office. My phone wasn't ringing off the hook.

During the playoffs that season, the Dallas Cowboys won the NFC championship game, and then two days later the Bears announced that Dave Wannstedt, the Cowboys' defensive coordinator, would be the next coach of the Bears. We were informed that Coach Wannstedt would be in the office for a few days and that he wanted to interview each coach. My meeting lasted five minutes. Basically, he said that he didn't know me and that he liked to have guys on his staff with whom he was familiar. And that was that. He was off to coach in the Super Bowl, so we all had to wait at least another week to find out if we were going to be hired. After my meeting, I called my wife and told her to take out the trunks and suitcases—we were about to move.

The day after the Cowboys won the Super Bowl, I received a phone call from Coach Wannstedt. I met him first thing in the morning, and he began by asking me to give him good reasons he should keep me on the staff. I replied that I'd show, rather than tell. So I drew up on the board the punt protection plan I would use. Halfway through my presentation, he stopped me and said, "Danny, do you want this job?" What a change of events! I immediately called Claudia and told her what had happened, and she was elated.

In Coach Wannstedt's second year, we made it to the playoffs as a wild-card team. This season was especially thrilling because, after ten tries, I finally had a winning season in the NFL. We won the wild-card game but lost in the divisional playoff game to my old 49ers team. Despite this success, our next two seasons were mediocre, and we failed to make the playoffs both years.

## Stress Relief

Early in our time together, I discovered in conversation that Coach Wannstedt was a Catholic, so after a few weeks I let him know that I went to the 6:30 a.m. daily Mass at Saint Mary's, near the Bears' facility. Most mornings he joined me, and we were back at work at 7:15. During this time I was also introduced to a wonderful priest of Opus Dei, Fr. Peter Armenio, who ended up becoming something of an informal team chaplain. He would hear the confessions of our Catholic coaches and give spiritual direction, even to our Protestant colleagues.

Coaching in the NFL is an intensely stressful job, especially in a large, football-crazy city like Chicago. The stakes are high; the money is huge; and the pressure is intense. Fortunately, in addition to going to daily Mass regularly and our sessions with Fr. Armenio, Dave and I began attending a nondenominational Bible study each Tuesday morning in the off-season that helped us relieve some of our stress by grounding us in the Word of God.

Being "too busy" is one of the most common reasons people—especially men—give for neglecting their spiritual well-being. But it's when we're busiest—with work or family or school or other responsibilities—that we need to make the strongest effort to make time for the Lord. I've found that not only do good spiritual habits, such as attending daily Mass and small-group discussions, help to relieve the stress of all the responsibilities weighing on me—they also really seem to multiply the time in my day. I'm more ready to get things done efficiently and professionally when my spiritual life is in order.

Even more importantly, giving time to the Lord each day helped me to keep everything in my life in the proper order. With all the craziness of the NFL life, it's vital to remember that family and faith come first. When those things falter, everything else follows. And when they're going strong, everything else follows.

That's why it was so important that Claudia and I had settled into a happy life in Chicago. Not only did we live near a wonderful parish where I established a men's prayer group, but the Marytown Franciscan Monastery and the National Shrine of St. Maximilian Kolbe were in the area. We were especially pleased that the monastery offered perpetual Adoration, and we participated often. These places, and the spiritual disciplines associated with them, were welcome respites from the intensity of my work with the Bears.

Chicago was also the home of my cousin, Auxiliary Bishop Alfred Abramowicz. I didn't know him as a child, but Claudia and I became close to him shortly after arriving in Chicago. We weren't Bishop Abramowicz's most interesting friends, though.

It turned out that Bishop Abramowicz had taken it upon himself to bring many Polish priests and seminarians to Chicago to learn English. He also founded a Polish house of studies for the archdiocese. All his connections to Poland led to him being the personal host for Cardinal Karol Wojtyla on his visit to Chicago! And when Cardinal Wojtyla became Pope John Paul II, he still stayed with my cousin when he was in town! The two were good friends until Bishop Abramowicz's death. In fact, as we'll see, their connection made it possible for me to meet the future saint years later.

## Homecoming

After my fourth year on Coach Wannstedt's staff, my contract was up for renewal. Something uncomfortable began stirring inside me. For one thing, my contract negotiations were at a stalemate. A few nights in a row Claudia and I went to Marytown to pray before the Blessed Sacrament. During my prayer, the Lord put on my heart that He had something else in store for me and that it was time for me to leave the Bears. I shared this with Claudia, who said she felt the same way. Neither of us had any idea what the next step would be, but we both knew it was time to move on.

Now that we had stepped out and made up our minds to leave the Bears with no job in hand, we really began to pray in earnest. One night my wife and I were praying and reflecting on what the Lord possibly had in store for us, when she felt a sudden connection to the Scripture passage about Jonah in the belly of the whale for three days (Jonah 2:1–2). After we spent some time meditating on this passage, we both concluded that the Lord was letting us know that something could happen within the next three days.

We went about our business and on the evening of that third day, I went to Marytown for Adoration. While I was there, Coach Ditka called. When I called him back, he informed me that he had just accepted the head coaching job for—you guessed it—the New Orleans Saints! And he wanted me to be his offensive coordinator. When I hung up the phone Claudia and I stared at one another in shock. Then we both began to pray, thanking the Lord.

The off-season before the 1997 season was very hectic for all of us in the Saints organization. After we watched all the game tapes from the previous year and examined the balance sheet, we determined that the Saints were not in good shape, on or off the field. We released some big-name players, which didn't sit too well with some of the other veterans, but it certainly got their attention.

We had a chance for stability at the quarterback position, but the Saints' management low-balled Randall Cunningham on their contract offer, and so he signed with the Vikings—whom he led to two straight playoff appearances. Meanwhile, in my three-year tenure in New Orleans we had seven starting quarterbacks: Heath Shuler, Doug Nussmeier, Kerry Collins, Danny Wuerffel, Billy Joe Hobert, Billy Joe Tolliver, and Jake Delhomme. As you might imagine, we never had a winning season.

As you also might imagine, all that losing led to some tension between me and Coach Ditka. Both of us are very, very competitive. On one occasion we were playing the Chargers in the Superdome before a packed house, and the game was very close. I ordered an audible to a toss play to take advantage of the Chargers' defensive formation. It would've worked perfectly, but the running back bobbled the toss, leading to a Chargers fumble return touchdown. Of course, Coach Ditka immediately got on my headset and screamed these exact words: "Danny, that was the worst call I have ever seen in the NFL!" I replied, "The worst ever?" He said, "Yes" and then turned off my microphone. That play changed the momentum of the game, and the Chargers went on to win.

That night I had a hard time sleeping, and I got up early the next morning to go into the office to watch the game tape. It turned out the play was wide open and probably would have gone for a score if executed properly. A few minutes later, Mike appeared in my office with a big cigar in his mouth. All he said to me was, "It was open, huh. Good call." And he smiled and walked out.

At one of Coach Ditka's early press conferences in New Orleans, he made the bold statement that if we couldn't turn this program around in three years, he should be fired. Well, after three years we hadn't turned the program around, and we were fired. I must say that I was relieved. Those three years were very difficult physically and emotionally, and I was just glad it was over. Moving on from that situation was a great blessing for me and my family.

## The NFL Lifestyle

People outside the NFL experience the thrills of the games on Sunday but don't realize the amount of time and preparation it takes to get ready for these games. Most coaches in the NFL are in the office during the season before 7 a.m. and often don't leave until 11 p.m. There's not much time left in the day to spend with family. Coaching can, as you can imagine, put a tremendous strain on marriages.

Different organizations and different head coaches have different routines, but my experience was pretty standard. The coaches would usually gather in the office in the early morning on Monday to examine that Sunday's game tape and grade each player's performance. Later the head coach would address the team, and we'd break the players into sections by position to watch game tape—both of themselves and of next week's opponent.

Tuesday was game-plan day for coaches, and players got to rest. We presented the game plan to the players on Wednesday morning and practiced that afternoon. At night, then, the coaches would do particular preparations for third-down situations. And then on Thursday evenings, we'd prepare short yardage and goal-line plays to present to the team on Friday morning.

Things finally settled down on Friday after practice, when coaches could take off—except offensive and defensive coordinators, who would finalize game-plan sheets, leaving the office in the early evening. Saturday would be either for last-minute details, or travel for away games. We'd play on Sunday and start it all over again the next Monday.

After sixteen games (and, if we were lucky, a few playoff games), the off-season responsibilities would begin, and our schedules would get a bit more normal. But we'd still have to prepare for the Senior Bowl, free agency, the scouting combine, the draft, mini camps, and training camp. All in all, the coaches would put in more regular eight- to ten-hour days in the spring and summer.

The NFL lifestyle is intense—especially during the season. In addition to all the time we'd put in to preparing the team, there was the constant pressure from fans and media, especially in football-crazy towns like Chicago and New Orleans. The fame and the glamour came with intense scrutiny.

It's so important to have a strong family and spiritual life to keep you anchored. It helped that our kids were grown; I don't know if I could have been an NFL coach while raising children. Claudia and I were very intentional about making time for one another and for the Lord—regular daily Mass, Adoration, small groups, and so on. Without the graces that come from putting Jesus at the center—as in that little diagram years ago, with the cross at the center of the circle—life can quickly feel out of control.

# CHAPTER 5

# DONUM DEI

After being let go by the Saints, I spent some quality time with Claudia, discussing whether I had a future in the coaching profession or whether God was calling me to something else. We both decided that we really needed to spend a lot of time in prayer for discernment. For several nights we went to the Adoration Chapel and we attended Mass daily. I decided to go to Mobile for the Senior Bowl and to do some networking to find out what opportunities might be available.

The first day there, I ran into Jon Gruden, who asked if I would be interested in the special-teams-coordinator job with the Raiders. I told him that I appreciated the offer and would be in touch in a few days. On my drive back to New Orleans, I had a gut feeling that I needed to research other job opportunities besides coaching, which I told Claudia when I returned. I ended up taking two more calls about special-teams jobs, but I just knew my heart wasn't in it.

## A New Course

One day Joe Canizaro, a long-time friend of mine and a very successful businessman, invited me to lunch to talk about my plans. He really caught me by surprise when he asked me to be the executive director of his family foundation. I insisted that I had no idea how to run a foundation, but he was very serious about his offer. I told him I wanted to talk with Claudia and pray about it and that I would be back in touch.

For the next few days, I spent much of my time praying and reflecting on my future. I needed to make sure that I was doing what God wanted me to do, not what I wanted to do. Even though it was very tempting to remain in the NFL, deep down I felt that the Lord wanted me to go in a different direction. I finally came to the conclusion that God wanted me to accept Mr. Canizaro's offer. Many of my coaching buddies thought I had lost my mind, but they respected my decision, and I remain good friends with many of them.

I was apprehensive about accepting the foundation position since it would be a totally new experience for me, but the Lord was telling me to trust Him and to "put out into the deep" (Luke 5:4). Claudia was at peace with our decision, and we both knew that the Lord was leading us to this new stage in life. She was also happy to have me around the house more often and free from the stress of coaching in the NFL. This transition was much easier for us because we did not need to make another move, and since we were already such good friends with the Canizaro family.

Soon after I joined the foundation, we changed the name to Donum Dei, which is Latin for "gift of God." At our first board meeting for the newly renamed organization, we determined that the majority of contributions moving forward would be given to Catholic endeavors. Through the generosity of the Canizaros, the Donum Dei Foundation had an impact all over the Archdiocese of New Orleans and beyond, from Catholic schools and hospitals to pro-life efforts and relief for the poor. Donum Dei was also instrumental in the constructing of Eucharistic Adoration Chapels throughout the New Orleans area. I was incredibly blessed to have been a small part of this work.

## A Special Trip

While I was president of the Donum Dei Foundation, there was one project in particular that profoundly impacted my spiritual life. The Canizaros had a special connection to Medjugorje, a village in the region of Bosnia and Herzegovina where many people believe the Blessed Mother has appeared regularly to visionaries.

The Vatican has yet to give a definitive statement on the authenticity of the apparitions. While Church authorities have generally discouraged officially organized pilgrimages that would presume that the visions are genuine, individual Catholics have not been forbidden to go to Medjugorje. In my experience there, the presence of faithful Catholics from all over the world made my visit a truly special moment in my spiritual life. The spiritual energy in the place was truly incredible.

Despite the international interest in the town, many of the facilities—for locals and visitors alike—were simply not in very good shape. The Canizaros wanted to use their foundation to improve life in the village. My job was to explore the area and get to know the local stakeholders who could tell us how we could do the most good. It was wonderful to meet so many interesting people who wanted to improve their village for everyone, including the thousands and thousands of guests they graciously host.

During our visit, we laid out plans to fund a new wing for the local public elementary school, a new medical clinic for locals and pilgrims, a radio tower to broadcast Catholic programming, and a public Luminous Mysteries mosaic. Upon returning home I presented all the plans to the Canizaros, and they agreed to fund every project. I can hardly describe how honored I was to have been trusted with the Canizaros' resources and to be able to help the people and travelers of Medjugorje. The entire experience was an incredible blessing.

The most amazing part of all is that the plans, permits, and construction took only a little more than a year—and they were under budget! Joe Canizaro and I went back to Medjugorje for the ribbon-cutting ceremonies. We even processed with the pastor, who was in full liturgical vestments, to the public school to bless each new classroom with holy water. We saw crucifixes hanging in every classroom and nuns teaching many of the classes. It was amazing and beautiful to see the Faith integrated into public life so fully!

## Meeting a Saint

Even though I was heavily involved with the operation of the Donum Dei Foundation, I still remained active in evangelization, speaking at many National Catholic Men's Conferences. Whenever I would speak at men's conferences, men would come up to me during the breaks and ask me where they could buy my book. Well, I didn't have a book—so they'd encourage me to write one.

I started to ask the Lord whether this was something I should do. After much thought and prayer, I decided to write a book about my personal spiritual-workout plan, using sports terminology and examples that would appeal to guys. (Some of my spiritual-workout plan appears at the end of this book.) I know the Dominican nuns who taught me in grade school and high school were laughing in heaven at the idea of my writing a book, but it ended up being fun — even if a little difficult at times. The title of the book, referencing my NFL career, was Spiritual Workout of a Former Saint.

Because of my Polish roots and the close friendship between Pope St. John Paul II and my cousin, I wanted to send a copy of my book to the Holy Father. So in August 2004, I mailed two copies of the book to Bishop Stanislaw Dziwisz, the Pope's private secretary, with a note explaining that I was Bishop Abramowicz's cousin.

Around that time I was planning to return to Medjugorje with my friend, Dr. Dan Jacobs, a medical doctor who advised on our clinic project, to check on the progress of the plans we funded. A few days before we left, though, a letter arrived from Bishop Dziwisz, thanking me for the books on behalf of the Pope. What caught my attention was the invitation I received: "If your travels ever bring you to Rome, please contact me and I will arrange a meeting with the Holy Father."

He included a phone number, so I called immediately, since it was early evening in Rome. Much to my surprise, the bishop personally answered the phone — in English! I was speechless at first, and then introduced myself. We carried on a conversation for a few minutes, and then I informed him that I would be in Rome with my wife and another couple in early November during our trip to Europe, and he told me to call him when I arrived. I couldn't wait to get home that night to tell my wife and to see the reaction on her face.

We traveled to Rome on November 2, 2004, and as soon as we got settled, I called Bishop Dziwisz. He instructed me to be at the Vatican at 10 a.m. two days later. I could hardly sleep the night before, so I got up early to do my morning prayers. I knew this was going to be a special day when I reflected on the meditation by John Paul II in the *Magnificat* prayer book, which included the line, "Everything is a gift of God"—*donum Dei*.

That morning, as we neared the entrance of the Paul VI Audience Hall, throngs of Polish people, all dancing and singing in Polish and dressed in festive garb, were waiting to enter. I figured that with all these people, we would never get to see the Holy Father personally. When the guards opened the gate, though, they checked our reservation and immediately led us to the very front of the stage, to five chairs just for us. I had goose bumps, and my heart was racing.

A few minutes later, the Swiss Guard marched out onto the stage, the doors opened, and the Pope entered in a large chair. He had an enormous smile as all the people cheered wildly. I began to cry as I thought about how proud my Babka and my grandfather, both of whom had been born and raised in Poland, would be that there was a Polish Pope—and that I had met him!

After the Pope spoke to everyone in Polish, we lined up to meet him, and I prayed for the Holy Spirit's guidance. As I approached him, I kissed his hand and introduced myself as Danny Abramowicz, cousin of Bishop Abramowicz. His face immediately lit up, and he hit me in the chest with his hand and said, "We loved him!" I then walked over to Bishop Dziwisz and introduced myself to him as well. Dr. Jacobs had bought a zucchetto, an ecclesiastical skullcap, which he gave to the bishop. He then went behind the Holy Father and exchanged that zucchetto for the one on the Pope's head!

Dr. Jacobs placed the Holy Father's zucchetto in a special case, and the moment I got back to the hotel I placed my blue blazer, touched by Pope St. John Paul II that day, safely in a garment bag. I have kept that jacket preserved to this day.

*CHAPTER 6*

# VAGABONDS

A year later, in 2005, we were living in a lovely home on the north shore of Lake Ponchartrain in the quaint town of Covington. This was going to be our retirement home. It was on three acres of land with many beautiful tall pine trees. We were less than a mile away from a Benedictine monastery, and a mile in the other direction was a Carmelite monastery of cloistered nuns. It was like heaven on earth for us. We could attend daily Mass at either monastery and join in their prayers whenever possible.

The only drawback was my fifty-mile commute into New Orleans. Some of the work I did for the foundation could be handled from my home, though, so I worked in the office three days a week and from my house the other two days.

Our oldest son, DJ, was living and working in New Orleans, and our pregnant daughter Stephanie, her husband, Stephen, and their son Dillon had recently moved to town as well. Our son Andy got married in June 2005 and was living in Los Angeles. Life in the Abramowicz family was looking good.

## Not Like the Others

I remember the evening in August 2005 when the hurricane warning for Katrina was announced. We had experienced evacuations in the past, so we knew enough to prepare the house, gather clothes for a few days, fill the car with gas, and buy some snacks and water for the slow caravan out of town. Our children in New Orleans joined us so we could travel together in the lighter traffic across the lake.

But because it was such a massive evacuation, we couldn't find a local hotel that could accommodate us. I prayed about what to do in this precarious position. Then a friend named Bobby John from Lafayette, safely inland in south-central Louisiana, called to invite us to his place to stay. It took us twice as long as usual to get there, but we were blessed to be in a safe place.

I don't have to tell you what happened next. We expected, as usual, to be free to return to Covington within a few days. But this time was different. Although Hurricane Katrina upended our lives as we never expected, we fared well compared with the devastation suffered by so many in our city.

After a full week in Lafayette, I knew we needed to make some other arrangements. My brother Joe called from Memphis, where he had evacuated, to tell me he had found an apartment complex that was renting units to hurricane evacuees on a month-to-month basis. We were blessed to be able to rent the last remaining two-bedroom unit.

Before leaving for Memphis, I drove to Covington with my son and son-in-law to see if our home had sustained any damage. Fortunately, the area had only wind damage. We were permitted to make a short visit, but there was no electricity, food, water, or gas, and many roads were impassable. When we finally arrived at the house, we noticed that two trees had fallen on our roof. Only one branch punctured the roof, though, so we sawed it off and patched the hole. Off we went, just hoping that the patch would hold until we could return, and not knowing when that would be.

After about a month in Memphis, we returned to Louisiana to begin the long clean-up process. When we pulled up in front of our home, my wife could not believe her eyes: the beautiful pine trees that had given us beauty and privacy were scattered all over our lot.

But now we had another option. Joe Canizaro recognized that New Orleans wouldn't get back to normal for quite some time, so he invited me to help out a new company he had acquired in Memphis. Claudia and I discussed the whole matter, and she was more than open to the move.

Every time Claudia looked out the window and saw all those beautiful trees in shambles, it was too much. She did not want to go through the expensive and time-consuming clean-up process; she just wanted out. Furthermore, both of our children in New Orleans and our son-in-law lost their jobs due to the disaster. We had planned to stay in Covington for the rest of our lives, but now, in a matter of weeks, we no longer had anything tying us to Louisiana.

## A Layover in Memphis

In October we closed on our home in Covington and were on our way to Memphis again. We were blessed to be able to find a house close to my new office and a wonderful parish, and things finally slowed down long enough for us to reflect on all that had transpired over the past four months. We were convinced that all of this was part of God's plan for us, and that we should make the best of it.

At the first Sunday Mass we attended at our new parish, Our Lady of Perpetual Help, we were impressed with the entire experience, especially with the number of people who introduced themselves and welcomed us. We were glad to see that they offered two daily morning Masses, and weekly women's and men's groups.

Not long after we registered in the parish, we became actively involved in these groups, which were a blessing for both of us. We each made friends individually, and we also started to social-ize as a couple. The experience of sharing our spiritual journeys together allowed us to form far deeper and more important re-lationships more quickly than we would have otherwise. This social and spiritual growth is why I have been involved in small groups for over thirty years, and why I continue to recommend them to other men (and women!).

I was even able to help the Diocese of Memphis organize its first men's conference. Although Memphis is a major city—the biggest in Tennessee and in the entire region—it has relatively few Catholics. With my experience in New Orleans and Chicago and along with a talented leadership team and the complete support of the bishop, we were able to put together a success-ful diocese-wide men's event that included speakers, Mass, and confessions. I'm so glad that the tradition we were able to start in our short time in Memphis continues to this day. In fact, I just returned from attending their Eleventh Men's Morning of Spirituality Conference—what a blessing!

When we moved to Memphis, though, Claudia and I sus-pected it wouldn't be permanent. Both of our dads were aging, and their health was slipping. They also both lived alone and would never leave Steubenville, so we knew we would eventually need to care for them.

One evening, just as we sat down to have dinner, my wife's sister called to tell us that their father, "Pepper," had been rushed to the hospital due to a heart problem. Claudia flew home the next day to be with him. After several days, doctors still didn't have a diagnosis, but Pepper had improved enough to be sent home. Things seemed to be moving along smoothly, but a few weeks later he was back in the hospital. We packed up the car up with enough stuff to stay for an extended period and drove north.

## "I Am Ready"

We spent the first few days back in Steubenville in and out of the hospital with Pepper. The Saturday after we arrived back home, we decided to go to the gym after Mass to get a good workout and clear our heads. I usually exercise briskly for about an hour, and, naturally, when I'm finished, I'm sweating and my heart rate is elevated. This particular morning, though, the sweating and the racing heart didn't stop after the workout ended.

On the drive home, I began to feel a heaviness in my chest. I didn't want to alarm Claudia, so when we got home I grabbed a Gatorade and went outside to see if things would settle down. But I only felt worse, so I went back inside and told her that something was wrong. She took one look at me, white as a ghost, and told me to get in the car immediately.

When we arrived at the emergency room, they rushed me inside, and, all of a sudden, lights were flashing and people were scurrying around. The next thing I knew, I was lying on a table in my birthday suit. They began poking IVs into me and hooking me up to machines. While all of this was taking place, a lady came up to me out of nowhere, placed a holy medal on my chest, and walked away.

I would like to share with you a very personal prayer that occurred to me as I lay on that table. For many years during my prayer times, I often wondered how I would respond when I faced death. I claim to know Jesus personally and to follow Him in my life, but what would my reaction be? Would I be angry, joyful, or sad?

I absolutely knew at that moment in the hospital that I was facing death. Just then the doctor said to me, "Mr. Abramowicz, you are having a heart attack, but we have it under control." I thought to myself, "Like hell you do." I leaned back on the table and prayed: "Lord, the timing is not good right now—I don't want to leave my wife with these two elderly dads to care for. Plus, I have these grandsons whom I would like to spend more time with. But Lord, if it be Your will, *I am ready.*" I was totally calm and at peace—not fearful of death.

As they were wheeling me into the catheterization room, the nurse asked me if I was ready, and I confidently said, "Yes, I am in the Lord's hands." It turned out my doctor was also my father-in-law's cardiologist. When he realized, he said with a calming smile on his face, "Didn't we just see each other this past Thursday?" I was awake enough throughout the stent-implant procedure to hear him say that my artery was 100 percent blocked, and that it was fortunate that I came to the hospital when I did. Afterward, the doctor told me that if I hadn't taken care of myself as I did, I probably would not have survived the heart attack. Once again, the Lord's hand was upon me.

A little while later I was resting in my bed, and, much to my surprise, a high school classmate of mine walked in. Dr. Pat Macedonia was at the hospital making his rounds when he heard that I was there. Word gets around fast in a small town! We started talking about our Faith and how the Lord had touched both of our lives. Although we grew up on different sides of Steubenville, we shared a bit of a troublemaking nature in high school. But now here we were, sharing how we were both trying to live out our Faith as Catholic men.

Never missing an opportunity to seed a men's ministry, I suggested that we start a men's small sharing group at the hospital. I told him that I would lead the group if he would recruit the men. Several weeks later, we held our first small-group meeting in the hospital with four doctors, one nurse, and me. It turned out that the nurse was on duty the day of my heart attack; here's an excerpt of a letter he sent me afterward:

Upon hearing your diagnosis, I felt compelled to come to your bedside despite the number of people already caring for you. Because of the activity in the room, I was unable to see your face; however, I noticed a gray color to your body and huge beads of sweat on your body. I knew at that moment you were walking a fine line between life and possible death if the treatment was delayed, or if you did not respond well to the treatment.

As I neared your bed everyone was preparing you for the cath lab, but I noticed no one was really talking to you. Their minds were preoccupied with saving your life. I then offered you a pat on the shoulder as I mustered out a few words of encouragement to you.

Now I know enough in my 12 years as an ER nurse to never make promises to patients because you don't know when someone's time is up. But I blurted out to you, "You'll be okay, Bud. You're in good hands here. It'll be okay."

I began to walk away, thinking in the form of a prayer, "What did I just say? God please help this man, don't let him die!" At that moment your voice caused me to turn around, and you looked at me with laser focus through all the chaos and said, "It's in God's hands now, whatever will happen is up to Him." Then you looked back at the ceiling and closed your eyes. Dumbfounded I said, "Yeah, you're right, you're very right!" Let me tell you, your comment stopped a few folks dead in their tracks. I'm not sure if their reaction was because of your faith, because you mentioned God, the calmness you displayed, or just that you would be okay with whatever happened. Most conscious patients in a life-threatening situation are really dying to hold on (pardon the pun). Perhaps they are not yet ready to go or maybe they never thought about death.

Dumbfounded, I left the room. I literally felt three inches tall after witnessing the amount of strength, courage, and peace you had just displayed at such a physically fragile time. This type of strength is different than physical strength, and very few individuals obtain it. I have to admit I felt weak, afraid, and inspired all at the same time. Here I was supposed to be trying to comfort you and you already had your mind made up; you were cool with whatever would be.

I share this to remind all of us that we witness to our Faith every moment of every day—even naked on a hospital gurney. There's always someone watching, and that someone may be profoundly affected by even the smallest sign of faith.

## Fathers' Farewells

I was released after only a few days, but Pepper's condition was not improving. For the next few weeks, they kept moving him from one facility to another for insurance reasons, and he was increasingly disoriented and frustrated. One morning they brought him his breakfast tray, and when they returned to pick it up, he had died. We felt that he had just given up on life. Pepper's death greatly impacted my dad because they were very close friends; as often happens in old age, my dad was realizing that all his friends were passing away.

Prior to Pepper's death we had begun to remodel his house. It was obvious to us now that we would need to relocate to Steubenville to take care of my dad, so we continued the remodel, now in order for us to move in and tend to my dad. We traveled back to Memphis to put our house on the market and to inform Mr. Canizaro that our move to Steubenville would be permanent. This brought to an end eight great years of working with Joe, but it was clear that the Lord had new work in store for us.

The house was ready for my dad to move in with us, but he wasn't ready yet. I started to visit him more often to make sure things were okay, and I noticed a slight physical and mental change in him: his balance and memory, previously so strong, had begun to slip. But one day when we went to visit him, I noticed a packed suitcase in the front room. My dad entered the room like a little kid and gently asked if he could move in with us.

For the first two weeks, he had a difficult time adjusting to being away from his own home. Women are so good when it comes to caring for others; my wife knew exactly what to do to help him. She drove down to his home and picked out some key pictures and pieces of furniture and brought them to our house to fix up his room and make him feel at home.

Everything was running smoothly until I came home one day to find my dad sitting in a chair staring out into space. I tried to get his attention but couldn't, so I immediately called 911. He spent a few days in the hospital and was released, but a week later he fell trying to get out of bed in the middle of the night and was disoriented. He went back into the hospital, where his doctor recommended that we put him in hospice and told us that he probably had five or six days to live.

Each day in hospice they told us that all the signs indicated that my dad would soon die. But on the fifth day, my dad woke up and asked for eggs and bacon. Apparently, the Lord wasn't ready for him yet! Two days later we moved him out of hospice and into long-term health care. He remained in this facility until his peaceful death six months later, on August 6.

Those six months were an incredible blessing for our entire family; we were all able to visit with him regularly, and our children and grandsons were able to spend time with him. Claudia and I visited him almost every day, but we couldn't help but notice the lack of family visitors to the other patients in the facility. It was so sad to experience this, but it also gave us the opportunity to reach out to these lonely seniors — and what a blessing they were! And at the very end, my brother and I were right at Dad's side.

My dad and Claudia's dad were WW II vets, close friends, and real characters. They went home to the Lord but will never be forgotten in Steubenville. Their overcrowded funerals (not to mention their wakes!) testified to the friendships they had formed during their long and well-lived lives on the Ohio River.

Although we dealt with many health issues during our short stay in Steubenville, as well as the deaths of our fathers and several aunts and uncles, the Lord continued to use me to evangelize Catholic men. Steubenville's bishop and I organized a men's conference, and as a result of this conference we organized a Fishers of Men small sharing group in one of the parishes. But the Lord had one more assignment for me during my time in Steubenville — the *Crossing the Goal* men's ministry.

## Crossing the Goal

For nearly a decade I have been privileged to serve on the board of directors for the Eternal Word Television Network—the largest Catholic media network in the world. Not long after I published my book, I was approached by EWTN about creating a TV miniseries based on it. After thinking and praying about it, we did the series and were pleased with the results.

In 2008 EWTN approached me again about doing a new series geared toward men. I told them I liked the idea, but I needed to take it to prayer to see what God wanted me to do. One evening in Adoration, the Spirit spoke to me very clearly in a question-and-answer format. I heard, "What do men like to watch?" "Sports," I answered. The questions continued: "What is the most popular sport?" "Football." "What are the most popular shows?" "*Sportscenter* and *NFL Today*." "Your show needs to be based on that format."

In developing the program, I wanted to accomplish two main objectives: to evangelize Catholic men and to establish a brand name for Catholic men's ministry. But before we could begin discussing a logo, we needed to come up with a name. Several of my friends and I couldn't find a name we liked, but Claudia came to the rescue with *Crossing the Goal*. Everyone loved it!

From the very beginning, our philosophy for *Crossing the Goal* was to harness the concept of the team for the honor and glory of God. Our mission was to evangelize men to help them become spiritually fit so they could cross over the goal into eternal salvation. Each series and its preparation was a team effort—from the content, to the talk titles, even to the team clothes we wore.

After one year of producing CTG on EWTN, we felt that we needed to take the show on the road, so we decided to host

CTG Catholic men's conferences in dioceses throughout the country. Our first effort in Columbus, Ohio, was a rousing success—they more than doubled attendance from the previous year, and a majority of the men went to Confession! The Holy Spirit clearly blessed the efforts of the Diocese of Columbus, the CTG organizing team, and the men who attended.

Our conferences presented a comprehensive program centered on the themes of conversion, transformation, and evangelization. Depending on the size of the crowd, we normally had twenty to thirty priests hearing confession throughout the day. This sacrament, along with the closing Mass, was the most powerful aspect of our conferences. After every event, priests would tell us that men went to Confession who hadn't done so in twenty-five years or more. What a blessing to have so many men return to full communion with the Lord and His Church! We would close out the day with Mass celebrated by the bishop. It is so powerful to hear and see hundreds, even thousands of men singing together, giving God the praise and the glory.

At a certain point, our team noticed that we were missing a key component of men's ministry: small groups. Each member of the CTG team had participated in small groups and experienced great spiritual growth from them for many years. So we decided to design a format for men's small groups called a Spiritual Fitness Workout. The basic format is ninety minutes long and consists of an opening prayer, an episode from one of our TV series, and smaller group discussions called "huddles." The meeting ends with each member writing down one action item for the next week.

As with all projects like this, it couldn't last forever. My teammates in this ministry moved on to other projects, and I needed a break as well. When it was all said and done, we taped 153 episodes of *Crossing the Goal* and led conferences all over the country.

I had been involved with the work of evangelizing men for over thirty years, and I really felt that I needed a sabbatical. But if you want to hear the Lord laugh, just tell Him your plans! A phone call here and an invitation there, and soon I found myself leading more Spiritual Fitness Workout programs in places such as Detroit and Minneapolis. My sabbatical was not only over, but things were more hectic than ever!

Through these new opportunities, though, eventually came a chance to settle down. I met some great people at these events who wanted to take the Crossing the Goal ministry to the next level. We assembled a new leadership team to revamp and professionalize our operations around ready-made online Spiritual Fitness Workout modules. And I could finally step away—at least a little bit.

## Settling Down — Finally — in Chicago

After our fathers' deaths, Claudia and I no longer had any reason to remain in Steubenville, and we both felt the Lord was calling us to move to Chicago to be near our children and grandsons. So, in March of 2011, that's what we did. We downsized to a two-bedroom apartment in a high-rise building. But the best part is that we're close to our grandchildren. Claudia helps watch the kids a few days a week, and I serve as chauffeur for sports and other activities. And we wouldn't have it any other way.

These years have brought some of the most fun and memorable moments of my life, such as the mud fight I had with my grandsons—after which, to my daughter's horror, we tracked all that mess into the house! I love playing football with the boys.

I'll never forget challenging my grandson Ward to a one-on-one game—similar to that first drill back in Saints camp many years ago. The first time I stopped him just short of the goal line, but the second time he pushed with all his might and scored. It was a simple moment of joy between a grandfather and his grandson.

Five years ago, I started a new tradition of making a retreat with the adult men of our family. The only thing I required was that they leave their cell phones at home and go to Confession. We have a great time together with prayer, daily Mass, fellowship, plenty of laughs, and great food. Each year we've added other guys from the extended family. Each of these retreats has been such a blessing; I would recommend them to all dads of adult children as a way to evangelize them without being too pushy.

As I have traveled around this country speaking at men's retreats and conferences, the number-one thing that weighs heavily on the hearts of fathers and grandfathers is that their adult children are not practicing their Catholic Faith—which makes it more likely that their grandchildren won't do so either. The number-one predictor of whether a child will continue in the Faith through adulthood is whether the father practices his Faith. This is why I am so passionate about men's ministry.

If we evangelize men, we evangelize families. And if we evangelize families, we evangelize the culture. And if we evangelize the culture, we evangelize the world.

# CHAPTER 7

# THE GAME PLAN

In order for me to organize my spiritual-workout program, it was first necessary to take a spiritual inventory of my life. I formulated this spiritual inventory around what I like to call God's winning formula of the four Ws. Following each series of questions is a brief reflection on how it applies to my experience.

## The Will of God — Conversion

"Not every one who says to me, 'Lord, Lord,' shall enter the kingdom of heaven, but he who does the will of my Father who is in heaven." (Matt. 7:21)

Questions to consider:
+ Do I follow the will of God in my life, or my own will? In other words, do I live according to my ways or God's ways?
+ Do I have Jesus Christ as my highest priority?
+ Do I have a personal relationship with Him?
+ Do I give God a fair share of my time?
+ Do I communicate with God through prayer?

In the past, I lived according to the lyrics of that old Frank Sinatra song: "I Did It My Way." Well, "my way" is not the way to heaven! God has created us with a free will, and with this free will we can decide either to follow His way or not. The will of the Father is that we follow His Son, and the only way that we can do this is to establish a personal relationship with Jesus. For many years, I knew who Jesus was, but I didn't know Him personally. He must be the center of our heart—our number-one priority. The only way we can accomplish this is by the power of the Holy Spirit.

## The Word of God — Transformation

"For the word of God is living and active, sharper than any two-edged sword, piercing to the division of soul and spirit, of joints and marrow, and discerning the thoughts and intentions of the heart." (Heb. 4:12)

Questions to consider:
- Do I read and reflect on God's word in Holy Scriptures?
- Do my family and I read the week's Scripture passages before attending Sunday Mass?
- Do I ever spend any time studying the Catechism of the Catholic Church?
- Do I even own a Catechism or a Bible?

In that dark period of my life, I am not sure if we even owned a Bible—and I know we didn't have a *Catechism*. Of course, it's obvious that I wasn't living in the Word of God because I wasn't even familiar with the Word of God. Consequently, there was no way that I could possibly know Jesus in a personal way. We have to spend time with people to get to know them! The only time I would even hear Scripture would be at Mass on Sunday, and it would go in one ear and out the other.

## Witness for Christ — Evangelization

"So every one who acknowledges me before men, I also will acknowledge before my Father who is in heaven; but whoever denies me before men, I also will deny before my Father who is in heaven." (Matt. 10:32–33)

> Questions to consider:
> * Do I witness on behalf of Christ by my words and actions, especially to my family?
> * Do I truly believe in the Real Presence of Christ in the Eucharist?
> * Do I live a life based on true faith and morals? And do I stand up for godly principles?

The sad thing was that I think I believed in the Real Presence a little bit, but I did not truly believe with all my heart. So there was no way that I could witness for Christ — period! As you saw, I was living my life based on the Faith and morals taught not by the Church but by the culture. And, of course, I was standing up not for godly principles but for worldly principles. What was so phony about me was that I would defend fellow men when I felt they were wronged, but I had turned my back on my Creator, whom I wronged every day.

## The Winning Crown — Eternal Salvation

"I have fought the good fight, I have finished the race, I have kept the faith. Henceforth there is laid up for me the crown of righteousness, which the Lord, the righteous judge, will award to me on that Day, and not only to me but also to all who have loved his appearing." (2 Tim. 4:7–8)

Questions to consider:
* Do I concentrate more on earthly possessions and rec-ognition than on the crown of eternal salvation?
* Do I look to Jesus as the Way, the Truth, and the Life?
* Do I realize that my salvation comes through Christ, or do I think that I can earn it or buy it?
* Do I really believe that Christ died for me personally?

As I look back now, I was grabbing for everything of earthly value — trying to accumulate as much wealth, status, and plea-sures as possible — but I never took into consideration that awe-some statement Jesus made in Mark 8:36: "For what does it profit a man, to gain the whole world and forfeit his life?"

## Spiritual-Workout Plan

The only way I can continue to grow in holiness is to commit to following a spiritual-workout plan faithfully. The key to spiritual growth is prayer, which equips us to battle the temptations of this world. In the Gospels, Jesus talks to His disciples about prayer, because He knows they can't survive without it, and neither can we. Also, the Scriptures tell us that Jesus often went off to pray either alone or with His disciples.

Each day for the past twenty-five years I have tried to be-gin my spiritual workout by attending early-morning Mass. The Eucharist is, after all, "the source and summit of Christian life" (*Lumen Gentium* 11). If I truly believe that the Eucharist is the Body, Blood, Soul, and Divinity of Jesus Christ, why wouldn't I want to receive Him daily? If we keep our bodies healthy by eating nutritious food, why wouldn't we partake of the spiritual nutrition of the Eucharist as often as possible? "Truly, truly, I say to you, unless you eat the flesh of the Son of man and drink his blood, you have no life in you" (John 6:53).

After Mass I come home, get my coffee, and spend about forty-five minutes in prayer, including reading and reflecting on the Scriptures—especially the ones I've just heard at Mass. In the same way that we build up muscles over time, I've slowly increased the amount of time I spend praying in the mornings as my spiritual strength grows. And now that I'm a retired grandpa, I have time to pray in the evenings as well.

The Catholic Church also offers us another beautiful way to honor the Lord in the Real Presence through Eucharistic Adoration. This is time spent silently before the Lord, venerating Christ in the tabernacle, or in a consecrated Host that is displayed or exposed in a monstrance on the altar. Some churches even have their own Adoration Chapels set aside for Perpetual Adoration, which means the Host is exposed continuously—twenty-four hours a day, seven days a week. Our parish offers Adoration every Thursday evening from 7 to 8 p.m., and Claudia and I try to make it every week.

The sacrament of Reconciliation is another important part of my spiritual-fitness workout program. I try to go to Confession monthly, but Claudia says I should go more often! This sacrament is not only a way for us to repent of our sins and receive the Lord's forgiveness, but it also produces a storehouse of graces.

As part of my prayers during the day, I include a Rosary and a Divine Mercy Chaplet, which I like to say while I'm doing my physical exercises. Claudia and I finish our day with evening prayers right after dinner. I also receive spiritual direction four or five times a year from my spiritual director so that we can discuss my strengths and weaknesses and I can get his feedback.

Whenever I pray, meditate, or reflect, I always have beside me my journal, in which I write personal notes of reflection, or Scripture passages that the Lord puts on my heart. This is also a time to write down aspects of my personal life that the Lord brings to my attention that I need to improve on with the help of the Holy Spirit. I've been journaling for many years and have often referred back to past journals as part of my prayer and meditation time. While doing so, I have experienced a sense of joy to see how much spiritual progress I have made over the years, but I also have been humbled when I realize that I still have a long way to go.

Lastly, we must all realize that our bodies are temples of the Holy Spirit, and therefore we should take care of them. Human beings are body *and* soul, together. Physical workouts have been and continue to be a big part of my life. I try to work out five or six times per week, including stretching, cardio fitness, and weight training. I am not training for the Olympics—just to maintain physical well-being. We must try to live a balanced life that consists of spiritual, physical, and mental fitness.

I must remind you that this spiritual-fitness workout program evolved over many years of practice. It gradually fell into place as I continued to grow in my faith over the years, although the basics were recommended to me by Buzzy, my original spiritual director and AA sponsor in New Orleans.

The most important part of any spiritual-fitness workout is the start. You must make up your mind that you want to strive to be the holiest person you possibly can be and then realize that you cannot accomplish this on your own and that you need the Lord's help, not to mention the help of fellow men just as committed as you are. Begin as I did, with small steps, and then gradually increase your spiritual workout as the Holy Spirit guides you. It takes a tremendous amount of commitment and perseverance because along the way you will face many obstacles from the evil one. Trust that the Holy Spirit will provide you with the strength to overcome all obstacles.

## Are You Ready?

Now, let's go back to the point when I was lying on the emergency-room table having a heart attack, and death was staring me in the face. If you remember, I told you that I was totally calm and at peace, and not fearful of death. Why did I feel this way while facing such a traumatic situation? The answer to that question is rather simple. I had been preparing for this inevitable event for years by staying committed to my spiritual-fitness workout program.

To end this book, I would like to pose a very important question. I ask you to answer it truthfully and then reflect on it before the Lord: If that were you on that emergency-room table having a heart attack, *would you be ready?*

> Watch therefore, for you do not know on what day your Lord is coming. But know this, that if the householder had known in what part of the night the thief was coming, he would have watched and would not have let his house be broken into. Therefore you also must be ready; for the Son of man is coming at an hour you do not expect. (Matt. 24:42–44)

# A WORD FROM CLAUDIA

Danny and I are the epitome of the saying "opposites attract." He is outgoing, talkative, and passionate about his work—an intensely driven leader. I tend to be introverted and easygoing—a thinker and a spectator. Although these differences have caused friction at times, that friction has, in turn, smoothed our rough edges. This peaceful coexistence didn't happen overnight! But over the span of fifty years, through prayer, the sacramental life, the Word of God, and the inspiration of the Holy Spirit—not to mention patient waiting, forgiveness, and acceptance—we now manage well as husband and wife, intent on traveling the road to heaven together.

Nevertheless, more growth awaits us both. The Lord is the one who says to us, "Closer, come closer to me. There is more in store for you. I want a polished product when we meet so my Father will be proud." These are enticing words that keep prodding us onward and hopefully upward toward our heavenly home.

It is so exciting to explore the narrow way that leads to heaven. No one but the Lord can so patiently and earnestly call us forward. He is encouragement along the way. He is wisdom for the ages. And He is love without end. The reward for enduring the difficult times and enjoying the good times is that we have come to know Jesus and to desire to be His friend for a lifetime.

I doubt there are too many people who have lived out St. Paul's famous words about love without missing a beat:

> Love is patient; love is kind; love is not envious or boastful or arrogant or rude. It does not insist on its own way; it is not irritable or resentful; it does not rejoice in wrongdoing, but rejoices in the truth. It bears all things, believes all things, hopes all things, endures all things. (1 Cor. 13:4–7)

And in all honesty, our marriage has been a mixed bag, with each of us producing the good, the bad, and the ugly. But by the grace of God, we have taken advantage of episodes of turmoil to see ourselves as we really are and to seek God for the strength to eliminate the negative and accentuate the positive.

If you are experiencing or have experienced difficulties in your marriage or in other relationships, do not despair. Your hope lies in Christ. He brings good out of bad and turns sadness into joy.

It is my hope in this epilogue to tell of the glory of God and what He has done for me, so as to fortify your hope and trust in Him amid life's challenges.

## Young Love

I grew up in Steubenville, Ohio, not far from Danny, although the Abramowiczes lived in the Polish part of town, and my family, the DiPrinizos, lived in the Italian part of town. We had different parishes and schools, too: Danny went to St. Peter's, and I went to St. Anthony's.

In second grade I inscribed into the wood of the classroom coat closet the initials "CD+JC" within a heart. My young class-mates couldn't figure out who my boyfriend was, but the secret I kept was that the initials stood for Claudia DiPrinizo + Jesus Christ. There is nothing like young love, and the memory lasts forever. The wisdom of the ages tells me that Jesus Christ, who branded those initials on my heart at my Baptism, has never stopped loving me and that His love is everlasting. It is the basic reality that we must know and believe.

Catholic education was the hallmark of my youth. Through-out my school years, the nuns did a wonderful job of teaching us about the love of Christ—because they were the love of Christ in action. Like many Catholic girls at the time, I would fashion a veil to see what I might look like as a nun. I even chose a religious name: Sister Helen, after my godmother.

The Dominican sisters who taught me displayed virtues that were excellent examples for the formation of youngsters. They introduced us to the basic prayers and truths of the Faith and prepared us to receive the sacraments. They laid the foundation for my spiritual life.

I find myself verbalizing this thought to my young grandsons: "You are building a foundation for your life in what you are learn-ing in the Faith; this is the first step in your development in the spiritual life. Don't leap ahead of yourself. Place one foot in front of the other and walk steadfastly forward. It is your vocation now to be students."

And as I write these words, I realize that it is good advice for each and every one of us always to be a student of Jesus Christ, for His knowledge is exceptional and inexhaustible. Our spirits will be robust if we absorb His teachings, and our lives will bear fruit.

## Young Love (Part 2)

I met Danny during my sophomore year of high school. He was a good friend of my dear cousin Tony D'Andrea, and they schemed together to have us meet. The big moment came when they made an appearance at a family celebration and Danny mustered up the courage to say hello. His twinkling blue eyes and chipped front tooth were too charming to resist! After clearing the hurdle of introducing himself, he followed up with frequent phone calls; he would make me laugh at his ridiculous jokes and smile at his, ahem, delightful singing.

These sweet overtures led to dates, movies, dances, and a lot of time just sitting around my house enjoying each other's company. During the evening visits, my dad would conveniently fall asleep on the living-room sofa, leaving us no choice but to sit around the kitchen table eating some of my mother's homemade dessert.

It was difficult being away from Danny when he was at college while I was still in high school. One summer I decided the long-distance relationship was too tough—and there was a nice young man in my school I was interested in. I told Danny it was time for both of us to move on. Almost before I hung up the phone, he was at my door begging me to change my mind! I did, and the rest is history!

When we married on August 20, 1966, I was only one year out of high school, and he was going into his senior year at Xavier. I was nineteen, and he was twenty-one—even then, it was pretty young to be getting married. But we had the support of friends and family, and while we were definitely nervous, we were mostly excited to be beginning our lives together.

A friend recently pointed out to me that Danny and I "grew up together"—not just in sharing a hometown, but in sharing our lives together from such an early age. Now, after fifty years of marriage, I can really appreciate the wisdom of that remark. This is true for all married couples, though, regardless of age. The process of making a life together—sanding off those rough edges that didn't seem to matter so much before—is always one of growing up. We really grew up during our first year of marriage, and we continued to grow during Danny's rookie year with the New Orleans Saints.

## Football Wife

Before I knew it, this kid I had married had grown into an overnight celebrity in a sports-crazy and very social city. I had never been outside of Steubenville, away from my family, or exposed to formal social events, but suddenly I found myself with a husband who was being constantly swept away to sign an autograph or to meet some important person. I had to adapt quickly and assume independence and responsibility for the duties of married life.

Somehow, with my hands and my heart full with children, I was able to remain calm while the storm clouds gathered.

At the same time, things obviously weren't going as I had expected them to. On the one hand, of course, Danny's success was a wonderful development. We didn't have to worry about money, and the attention was pretty enticing. But his unpredictable and intense schedule made keeping control of our shared life an ongoing struggle. We went from zero to 60—from an apartment in Cincinnati to being a star in New Orleans—really quickly

Further, during the early years of our marriage I experienced great homesickness for my family and the connectedness of my old neighborhood, school, and church. In this big, cosmopolitan city I felt not just alone, but uncomfortable and even unworthy.

I only had a high school diploma, but we were becoming a part of the elite of New Orleans. I was feeling unloved and also un-noticed, especially compared with tight-knit Steubenville.

At home, I was popular with friends and within my family, but in New Orleans, Danny became the star attraction in our shared life. In addition to being lonesome, I was jealous that I did not share the spotlight with him. Danny was with the other players so much, night and day, while I was alone in a strange city with our new baby. And as our family grew, I would always be referred to as "Claudia and the kids"—never just "Claudia." I felt that I didn't have an identity of my own. I was beginning to wonder if the end of my story could ever read: "and they lived happily ever after."

But God sees all things, knows all things, and has the rem-edy for all things. He puts in place people—friends, relatives, neighbors, acquaintances, and even strangers—who help Him deliver help to us. He knows when danger abounds, and it is His desire to save us. And that, I feel, is exactly what happened.

We made some wonderful friends in New Orleans, including some who were very religious and prayed a lot. One of these prayer ladies invited me to attend a retreat at a house called the Cenacle not far from our home. After a few retreats at the Cenacle, I came to appreciate the simplicity there—the gentle-ness of the sisters and the quietness of the environment—and I decided to re-create that in my home. In a corner of the living room, I set up my "prayer chair."

I received a tremendous healing during one of my prayer ses-sions when I read in Scripture the simple truth that God loves me. Of course, I had heard this before, but I never really felt and understood the importance of this truth. This was and is the most fundamental reality of which I needed to be certain.

And furthermore, it was impressed upon me in this prayer that He loves me just the way I am—and that the way I am is very important to Him.

Honestly, I am no match for the dynamic personalities of the world, but I have come to believe that I am loved by and important to God. This was exactly what I needed to know during my struggles in New Orleans.

## The Grateful Wife of a Grateful Alcoholic

In marriage there are many stumbling blocks and stepping-stones. We were blessed to encounter a difficult experience that was both: the disease of alcoholism. When Danny told me he was an alcoholic around the fifteenth year of our marriage, I could not believe it. Danny's drinking and behavior seemed no more or less problematic than what I knew and saw while growing up. So, if these other people were not alcoholics, how could he be? When I thought of an alcoholic, I thought of a man literally lying in a gutter, not a good employee and doting father like Danny.

Yes, he did some stupid and shameful things, and we would have arguments when he came home drunk. Yes, I spent many nights crying myself to sleep—so many that I went to seek help because I thought I was to blame. When my therapist asked why I hadn't left Danny, I was confused because through the arguments and the tears I could still see the good in him. He loved his children, was a good provider, and was closely involved in family life. But then there was the other side of the coin. I struggled with what to do.

Obviously I did not divorce him, but the truth was that over the course of several years he had eroded the bond of trust between us. The task of reestablishing trust is both a leap of faith and a one-day-at-a-time experience. When Danny first stopped drinking, every time he arrived home, I would greet him with a kiss — in order to catch a whiff of his breath. Any time he was out late, I would get suspicious, and his get-togethers with old buddies would worry me.

Eventually, two things brought lasting peace: time, and the realization that, ultimately, Danny was in charge of his own life. I couldn't change him all by myself, and placing that burden on myself only made the process of rebuilding trust more difficult. Through time, though, the worrying and the suspicion faded because, with the Lord's help, Danny was putting himself back together.

Many succeed in rebuilding trust after a crisis in a marriage, but many fail in trying. We are fortunate and blessed that Danny is now living a life of sobriety, and we have been able to reestablish the trust that is the foundation of marriage.

## My Kind of Town

Our first family move since going to New Orleans was to Chicago, when Danny took the special-teams job with the Bears. Everything was great, though I missed my prayer sisters immensely. But God in His goodness led me to Marytown in Mundelein, not far from where we lived. To this day, perpetual Adoration continues there. What a blessing to be able to sit in the presence of the Lord, day and night!

In addition to personal renewal, Marytown provided a renewal of my love of the Catholic Church and of Mary, the Immaculata, as St. Maximilian Kolbe calls her. The renewed relationship with the Lord that I experienced in New Orleans was a result of the Catholic Charismatic Renewal and my Baptism in the Holy Spirit through that movement. At that time of my life, the emphasis was on the working of the Holy Spirit in my life, the power of prayer, and inner healing. I always loved the Catholic Church, but I didn't realize the depth of beauty and grace that was present in the Eucharist, the other sacraments, and the invaluable intercession of the Saints. I was now feeling and seeing the full power of the Catholic Church. I was becoming well rounded in my relationship with God, standing on His Word and being healed.

During our five years in Chicago, I also met many wonderful, courageous, and determined coaches' wives who knew the value of sticking together. Jan Wannstedt, the wife of the head coach, saw to it that the wives supported each other, so that we did not find ourselves stranded by the strenuous hours that our husbands kept. We would share meals while our husbands were traveling, sit together at games, and put on workshops for women to learn about football. I learned so much during these years about camaraderie and the importance of good leadership in the workaday world — not to mention generosity of spirit, patient endurance, and fortitude.

## Home Again

After a return to New Orleans and a stopover in Memphis, we finally returned to Steubenville. The move was such a blessing as we were reunited with our childhood home, family, and friends; plus we were able to take in the scenic beauty of the Ohio valley and engage in many activities at the Franciscan University of Steubenville.

But before we could enjoy all of this, Danny had a heart attack. As he was whisked away to surgery, I was taken to a waiting room where all I could do was pray over and over again these words from the Liturgy of the Hours: "God, come to my assistance. O Lord, make haste to help me." Amid all the busyness, an amazing event occurred: one of the hospital secretaries—Danny's former classmate—heard over the dispatch that he was in the ER and quietly slipped into the ER, where she softly laid a medal on him, said a prayer, and left.

It turned out, thankfully, that our Lord still had more work for Danny to do—or, more precisely, for Danny and I to do together.

## Settled, but Still Growing

Really big blessings flowed when, after the death of our fathers, we discerned that we should move to Chicago to serve our daughter and her family. With both parents working and three youngsters to tend to, we didn't want the children's care to be in the hands of strangers, and we wanted to spare the parents the expense of hiring a nanny. So, in the middle of a Chicago winter, our moving van arrived to unload a houseful of furniture into a two-bedroom apartment.

Somehow it worked, and our new home became a beautiful place to enjoy a new chapter of our life, one that would enmesh our lives with those of our children and grandchildren. In today's society, young families work very hard just to make ends meet. It is a blessing to have the desire, health, and wherewithal to help tend to three young boys. God is meeting the needs of this family and at the same time providing Danny and me with precious moments to support their development through words and actions. What a privilege to participate in their lives!

Even though our days are action packed (three boys will do that!), we have been able to enjoy a more serene and simple lifestyle than we have in many, many years. Our life is centered on our Catholic Faith: Mass, prayer, Scripture, Adoration, and family. We remind ourselves often of why we are doing this—we want to be obedient to the will of God to the best of our ability. Sure, it is tempting to escape the extreme winters in Chicago or to "retire" to some deserted place, but God's will rules. We want to be obedient to Him in the big and little activities of daily life.

Our life together has been one of constant change, but now, finally, we feel settled—until God tells us otherwise! Changing course not only becomes easier as our trust in God increases; it also enhances that trust by reminding us of our dependence on Him. And in Him, all things are possible.

I hope these words are encouraging for you. In this phase of my life, I am enjoying a personal relationship with Jesus that has been growing for many years. Even though perfection is elusive, it is the grasping that allows me to snatch precious bits of hope for a glorious future with Jesus in heaven when He calls. I hope we will all meet there someday with our families and friends in tow. Like those big parties back in Steubenville, it will be a blast of joy and excitement that none of us will want to miss—except this time it will never, ever end.